Better Ways to Better Relationships in the Church

Also by Thomas G. Kirkpatrick

*Small Groups in the Church:
A Handbook for Creating Community*

*Communication in the Church:
A Handbook for Healthier Relationships*

Better Ways to Better Relationships in the Church

Guidelines for Practicing Humility, Experiencing Empathy, Feeling Compassion, Showing Kindness, Expressing Appreciation, and Doing Justice

Thomas G. Kirkpatrick

WIPF & STOCK · Eugene, Oregon

BETTER WAYS TO BETTER RELATIONSHIPS IN THE CHURCH
Guidelines for Practicing Humility, Experiencing Empathy, Feeling Compassion, Showing Kindness, Expressing Appreciation, and Doing Justice

Copyright © 2021 Thomas G. Kirkpatrick. All rights reserved. Except for brief quotations in critical publications or reviews, no part of this book may be reproduced in any manner without prior written permission from the publisher. Write: Permissions, Wipf and Stock Publishers, 199 W. 8th Ave., Suite 3, Eugene, OR 97401.

Wipf & Stock
An Imprint of Wipf and Stock Publishers
199 W. 8th Ave., Suite 3
Eugene, OR 97401

www.wipfandstock.com

PAPERBACK ISBN: 978-1-7252-9993-1
HARDCOVER ISBN: 978-1-7252-9994-8
EBOOK ISBN: 978-1-7252-9995-5

05/17/21

New Revised Standard Version Bible, copyright 1989, Division of Christian Education of the National Council of the Churches of Christ in the United States of America. Used by permission. All rights reserved.

Contents

Acknowledgments | vii

Introduction | ix

Chapter 1   Practicing Humility | 1
Chapter 2   Experiencing Empathy | 19
Chapter 3   Feeling Compassion | 46
Chapter 4   Showing Kindness | 73
Chapter 5   Expressing Appreciation | 87
Chapter 6   Doing Justice | 103

Bibliography | 127
About the Author | 137
Index | 139

Acknowledgments

I am deeply grateful to the following people:

Social science colleagues whose research on relationships I've "translated" for use by congregations and their leaders.

Dr. Gordon S. Jackson, for his friendship and professional editorial expertise.

Rev. Dr. Duncan S. Ferguson, for his advice and support in finding a publisher for this book.

Matthew Wimer and his Wipf and Stock editorial and publication teams.

Members of two support groups, one personal and one professional, for creating a quality of relationships that matters most in my life.

And especially for members of my family, who are the primary source of better ways to better relationships in our lives over the years. It is to them that I dedicate this book: to my wife, Carol; my brothers and their spouses, Larry & Margie, Steve & Rhonda, and Ed & LeAnn; and my children and their partners, Matt & Lisa, Michele (Capri), Chris, and Juliann & Lawrence.

Introduction

A mid-sized congregation received a $50,000 bequest from the estate of a long-term member. This was the third such bequest in recent years. The congregation decided to use monies from the first bequest for deferred maintenance of its building, including tuckpointing its brick walls and refurbishing its stained-glass windows. Monies from the next bequest were used to remodel the fellowship hall, including an outdated kitchen. The congregation was deeply appreciative of these bequests and everyone was pleased with how the bequests were used.

Controversy arose, however, over how to use its recent bequest. Most options discussed by the board centered on using the new monies for additional building improvements—until the congregation's outreach ministry team met to discuss its recommendations. Heated debate surfaced among team members until Alex spoke. Alex was highly respected in the congregation and its most wealthy member. He rarely spoke up in meetings, but he decided to express his frustration with where the discussion was going this time. He said, "I've supported the use of our previous bequest funds for necessary building improvements. However, the building is now in good shape, and I think we've spent enough money on ourselves. In fact, *what is the clubhouse for if not to do ministry?*"

Alex's surprising and quite unexpected comment forever changed the mindset and direction of the congregation. It changed the dynamics of conversation and transformed relationships among team members, the board, and members of the congregation. Here was a quiet, humble team member showing empathy, compassion, and kindness for outsiders. His recommendation was rooted in a sense of justice and appreciation for people outside

INTRODUCTION

the congregation who needed the church's good fortune more than it did. It had enough for itself—and for those beyond its walls.

* * *

A local United Churches council decides to sponsor a town hall meeting to address protests against racial injustice by prominent professional athletes in its community. The mayor, a member of one of the faith communities with ties to local sports teams, is asked to moderate the meeting. Fans, athletes, and owners of several sports teams are invited to speak. Some fans show up with signs denouncing players for kneeling to protest racial injustice during the singing of the national anthem. Others display signs supporting Black Lives Matter protests. Tempers flare between fans supporting the right of players to protest and those feeling frustration with what they perceive as players' disrespect for the American flag. Shouting and jeering continue as the mayor begins the forum with an opening statement supporting the right of players to protest racism in America while also citing polls showing a growing number of fans are boycotting games resulting in declining game attendance and loss of revenue for team owners. She shows empathy for everyone's interests, calling for a compassionate understanding of each other's feelings and a fair, even-handed approach to a complicated, many-layered social issue.

The mayor then calls on an angry fan in a calm, kindly manner with grateful appreciation for their passion. In response, the fan poses a question with tolerance and curiosity rather than with hate and disgust: "I agree that systemic racism in America is a social evil we must all face together. Why, though, can't players find a different method of protest that seems more patriotic?" To which a player responds, "I don't see myself being unpatriotic at all. How can we take pride in a nation of liberty and justice for all when there's inequality and injustice for so many? I'm frustrated that you take my act of protest differently than I intend." A potentially volatile situation begins to turn into one of civility as empathy, compassion, kindness, appreciation, and fairness temper frustration, hate, anger, disrespect, and intolerance. During this era of racial protests, relationships begin to be transformed between people with opposing points of view, and impetus is sparked for churches and citizens to face and deal with racism in their community.

INTRODUCTION

* * *

These two scenarios could have had different, all-too-common outcomes. Many such controversies result in unhealthy relationships and communication breakdowns. People's frustration with one another can lead to blaming and angry harangues. Conversations spiral out of control as careful listening gives way to misunderstanding and supportive relationships are threatened by defensiveness. What can transform relationships gone awry? How can relationships be built, repaired, and restored so that they flourish and thrive? What are better ways to better relationships?

The way these scenarios unfold reveals ways to create healthier relationships—practices that have the power to transform relationships for the better:

- Practicing humility
- Experiencing empathy
- Feeling compassion
- Showing kindness
- Expressing appreciation
- Doing justice

None of these practices is a surprise, of course. They are rooted in relationship science and religious traditions along with a variety of philosophical, psychological, and cultural viewpoints. For example, such practices from the Judeo-Christian tradition include justice, kindness, and humility (see Mic 6:8). Likewise, a list of core values or character strengths in the New Testament book of Colossians includes compassion, gentleness, patience, and gratitude. Empathy is demonstrated in Jesus' parable of the Good Samaritan. Indeed, there is a wide array of practices found in a variety of perspectives that have the power to make our relationships flourish.

Social science researchers identify similar positive social behaviors. Indeed, "positive emotions have long been studied as markers of people's overall well-being or happiness."[1] A literature review of the texts of influential religious and philosophical traditions by Katherine Dahlsgaard identifies six sets of core strengths and positive social practices:

- Wisdom and knowledge (cognitive strengths)

---

1. Cohn and Fredrickson, "Positive Emotions," 13.

INTRODUCTION

- Courage (emotional strengths)
- Humanity (interpersonal strengths)
- Justice (civic strengths)
- Temperance (strengths protecting against excess)
- Transcendence (strengths of connection and meaning)[2]

Among twenty-four specific practices are religiousness, close relations, modesty, kindness, appreciation, gratitude, and fairness.

And while not the focus of this book, it is worth noting that most people around the world abhor leaders and members of society whose behaviors include:

- Arrogance and egomania
- Bigotry and hate
- Incivility and hostility
- Intolerance and indifference
- Bullying and abuse
- Injustice and unfairness
- Cruelty and evil

Ultimately, such negative social behaviors lead to relational breakdowns, religious extremism, intellectual chaos, political instability, and cultural disadvantage.

Fortunately, *most congregations and faith communities are eager to help people transform their relationships for the better.* Wide-ranging topics to consider include numerous transformative practices. It is not feasible, however, to satisfactorily address all such topics in a single book. So, this book targets six topics to create healthier relationships and repair relationship breakdowns in our congregations and faith communities: *practicing humility, experiencing empathy, feeling compassion, showing kindness, expressing appreciation, and doing justice.* You'll find chapters on each of these topics.

It is also possible to offer wide-ranging advice on these topics. Again, it is necessary to limit the scope of our inquiry. So, the *goal of this book is to provide some practical guidelines that can go a long way in helping people be more effective in how they transform relationships for the better in their*

---

2. Peterson and Park, "Classifying and Measuring Strengths of Character," 27.

INTRODUCTION

congregations and everyday lives. In short, you'll find practical wisdom in each of these six areas that will strengthen your relationships at home, at work, in congregations, and in society.

Overview of This Book

Here's what you'll find in each chapter:

- *Real-Life Scenarios*
- *Sensible Guidelines*
- *Practical Applications*
- *Suggestions for Further Study*

Further resources include extensive chapter footnotes and a bibliography and index at the back of the book.

You may adapt this book's content and resources to a variety of religious communities, learning audiences, work contexts, and educational programs. It is geared particularly for clergy, laypersons, denominational leaders, continuing educational planners, professors, students, and scholars. However, business and community leaders, nonprofit organizations, clinicians, consultants, and professional speakers will also find it useful. Insights are drawn from the latest research by relationship and social scientists on each topic. Wisdom gleaned from this research is translated into practical guidelines for transforming relationships gone awry, into relationships that flourish.

As this book was completed and goes to press, we are facing four momentous challenges as a human family: recovery of democracy, systemic racism, climate change, and a global pandemic. To help meet such challenges, the six topics of this book could not be more vital or essential. I hope the guidelines presented in the chapters that follow offer some practical ways to enrich and deepen relationships in your congregation and everyday life.

Chapter 1

Practicing Humility

Pride makes us artificial and humility makes us real.
—Thomas Merton

What does the Lord require of you but to do justice, and to love kindness, and to walk humbly with your God? —Micah 6:8

Goldie, Luis, and their young daughter Alexis rent a new home and look forward to getting to know their neighbors. On moving day, the couple across the street, Fidel and Rose, introduce themselves, welcome the family into their neighborhood, and invite them to visit their faith community sometime. Greetings are exchanged and the couple leave a ready-to-eat meal prepared by their congregation's deacons for their new neighbors.

After getting settled into their new home and grateful for their neighbor's hospitality, the newcomers invite Rose and Fidel over for dessert. The conversation is wide-ranging, easy-going, and seems to go well—until the couple returns home.

"What do you think about our new neighbors?" asks Fidel.

"Well, I really like Luis and Alexis, but Goldie—not so much," comments Rose.

"What do you mean?" inquires Fidel.

"Well, Goldie seems really full of herself and I find myself getting bored with our conversation."

"Yes, I know what you mean. And Luis hardly says a word." Fidel continues, "He seems reluctant to speak up and tends to put himself down when he does. I feel sorry for Luis and Alexis if that's the way they usually communicate. I wish they were more down to earth."

Rose concludes, "I might like to get to know Luis and Alexis better, although I'm not sure I'm up to the challenge. Hopefully, things will improve over time and we'll develop a good relationship."

To which Fidel adds, "Perhaps so. And if they visit our congregation there'll be opportunity for other people to connect with them."

This scenario demonstrates how having an inaccurate self-assessment can be a barrier to developing a satisfying relationship. In this chapter we will see why Goldie's exaggerated view of herself and Luis's underestimation of himself may negatively affect their ability to form healthy relationships in their new community. We will see how practicing humility, with its accurate, healthy view of one's self-worth and self-esteem, can positively impact our relationships. So, here are six sensible, practical guidelines that can significantly enrich the relationships in your congregation and everyday life. These best practices for cultivating humility will give you the power to transform your relationships for the better.

Guidelines for Practicing Humility

1. Think of Humility as a Multifaceted, Positive Social Behavior That Reflects an Accurate Self-View, Modest Self-Importance, and Appropriate Other-Centeredness.

Humility is often viewed negatively and associated with weakness, with a sense of unworthiness and insignificance, with having a low opinion of oneself, and with having low self-esteem and self-worth. However, Brazilian lyricist and novelist Paulo Coelho de Souza says, "Let us be absolutely clear about one thing: we must not confuse humility with false modesty or servility."

Similarly, as psychologist June Price Tangney points out, "in the theological, philosophical, and psychological literatures humility is a rich, multi-faceted construct, in sharp contrast to dictionary definitions that emphasize a sense of unworthiness and low self-regard. Specifically, the key elements of humility seem to include:

- an accurate assessment of one's abilities and achievements (*not* low self-esteem, self-deprecation)

- an ability to acknowledge one's mistakes, imperfections, gaps in knowledge, and limitations (often in relation to a "higher power")

- openness to new ideas, contradictory information, and advice
- keeping one's abilities and accomplishments—one's place in the world—in perspective (e.g., seeing oneself as just one person in the larger scheme of things)
- a relatively low self-focus, a "forgetting of the self," while recognizing that one is but a part of the larger universe
- an appreciation of the value of all things, as well as the many ways that people and things can contribute to our world."[1]

So, humility is not a negative behavior, associated with weakness, with low self-esteem, or with an underestimation of one's worth, abilities, or accomplishments. In contrast to the current behavior of Goldie and Luis, it is neither self-enhancing nor self-deprecating. Rather, it is a positive behavior associated with having an accurate, healthy view of one's self-worth, self-esteem, abilities, and achievements.

In addition, it is different from both false modesty and narcissism. Psychologist John Neafsey points out that true humility is part of being authentic: "It is grounded in the truth of who we are. It does not exaggerate our importance or abilities, but neither does it diminish our goodness or gifts."[2] Neafsey adds: "Humility should not be confused with low self-esteem or neurotic feelings of inferiority, because these too are not based on an accurate appraisal of the truth of who we are. True humility is not based on disparaging or diminishing ourselves. It is grounded in a right love for ourselves as we actually are."[3]

My wife has a learning disability that significantly affected her self-esteem. It severely limited her early-learning ability to spell and to read and led her to conclude that she was a "dumb blond." Years later when our son was diagnosed with a similar brain-sequencing learning disability, it dawned on my wife that she simply learns differently than others, rather than that she is "dumb."

In the Judeo-Christian tradition, Jesus pairs the imperative to *love our neighbor as ourselves* in Matthew 22:37–40 with the Hebrew Shema's commandment *to love God with our whole being* in Deuteronomy 6:4–5. This joining presumes that we have an accurate, positive, balanced, and healthy view of ourselves and others. Rather than a false modesty with its

---

1. Tangney, "Humility," 485.
2. Neafsey, *Act Justly, Love Tenderly*, 104.
3. Neafsey, *Act Justly, Love Tenderly*, 105.

tendency to lower our self-esteem by underestimating our capabilities, or a narcissistic grandiosity with an exaggerated sense of self-importance, overestimation of our abilities, and neglect of others, we can learn to view ourselves and others positively, accurately, and appropriately—in a word, with *humility*. This shift by Luis and Goldie has the power to transform their relationship with Rose and Fidel for the better. It also increases the likelihood of creating friendships with other neighbors and with members of a faith community or other organization they may seek to join. The practice of humility with its accurate self-assessment, modest self-importance, and appropriate other-centeredness is integral to creating healthier relationships with others. We love others *as ourselves*! In short, this three-way connection for people of faith between love for God, for self, and for others creates a healthy three-way relational love affair!

How, though, do we learn to balance self-love with love for others? The messages we learn about ourselves early in life are particularly formative. To our detriment, too often in our early childhood education we get back assignments with the number of wrong answers circled in red ink at the top of the page when we can just as well see the number of right answers circled in green ink. Moreover, all-too-often faith communities teach children to put others ahead of themselves or to count others as more important than themselves.

Unfortunately, these kinds of learning experiences can lead to lower estimations of our worth, importance, and performance than is accurate. It may partially explain how Luis became reticent to speak up and tends to put himself down. Knowing the number of correct answers on an assignment can be a much more accurate measure and nurturing message than focusing on the number of wrong answers. Likewise, when we learn to love our neighbors *as ourselves*, it need not be a question of who is more important. We need not choose between selflessness and selfishness. This perspective also helps guard against arrogance, on the one hand, and indifference on the other. Even though Rose finds Goldie "boring," she can guard against selfish indifference and arrogance by being gracious enough to patiently support Goldie as she finds her way in a new community. She can set her boredom aside long enough to offer acts of kindness that show concern for Goldie's well-being.

The three-way love perspective mentioned above means that everyone in a relationship is treated with equal value and worthiness, with the same dignity and respect. Healthy relationships are created with both-and mutuality and balance rather than with an either-one-or-the-other dichotomous mentality. Thus, even as we acquire a healthy love for ourselves by receiving accurate feedback and affirming messages from others, ourselves and God, we create healthy relationships with others by showing concern for their well-being and by giving and receiving messages of truth and grace, affirmation and appreciation, help and challenge. Balance and mutuality flourish: healthy self-love both creates and is created by healthy relationships with others, and healthy relationships with others both create and are created by healthy love of ourselves.

In religious communities, annual performance reviews of employed leaders that are "gift-centered" can be much more accurate and helpful than reviews that are "problem-centered." They continuously discern, identify, and celebrate a person's gifts and ask, "How is our pastor using her gifts for ministry?" rather than asking, "What is she doing wrong or poorly?" It is the difference between "caught you being good" and "caught you being bad." Gift-centered performance reviews focus more on what is appreciated about the spiritual leader's performance and less on what is not liked or is found lacking. It means that areas for improvement or challenges to be faced are discerned and seen in relation to her particular giftedness—for the purpose of nurturing her toward all that God is calling her to be, not in relation to some standardized template of good pastoring, not on overcoming weaknesses that are unlikely to change because God has instead called her to be a different kind of spiritual leader.

Findings from Research

Humility, as an accurate assessment of our abilities and achievements, appears to be a relatively rare human behavior. It may even be antithetical to our human nature. For example, our tendency toward self-enhancement is commonplace.[4] We tend to accentuate the positive and remember our successes, on the one hand, and deflect the negative and blame others for our failures and wrong-doing, on the other. These tendencies are shaped early in life and vary with our interpersonal, social, and work situations, however. For example, we may show modesty more with friends than strangers. Social science research finds that some degree of humility may be beneficial

---

4. Van Tongeren and Myers suggest that humility is rare and difficult because people are driven to perceive and present a positive self-image with self-enhancing bias blind spots in "A Social Psychological Perspective," 151–54.

because people like and feel less threatened by others who are moderately modest about their accomplishments. Conversely, boastful and arrogant behavior such as "tooting our own horn" is often responded to negatively. It is what makes Goldie's behavior such a challenge for Fidel and Rose in their desire for healthy neighborly relationships.

Research also shows that tendencies towards self-enhancement, grandiosity, and narcissism are troublesome in our interpersonal relationships. People who lack modesty, for instance, tend toward physical aggression more than those who are more modest. Likewise, narcissistic people are overly sensitive to interpersonal slights, prone to anger, and less forgiving. Conversely, healthy humility inhibits anger and aggression, and fosters forgiveness. It also shares credit without seeking undue attention and offers praise without conveying a sense of superiority.

Social scientists also find that an accurate assessment of oneself, neither unduly favorable nor unfavorable, is important to our psychological and physical well-being. Excessive self-focus, for example, is associated with increases in depression, anxiety, stress, phobias, guilt, and shame. A "forgetting of the self" in the sense of having a balanced self-consciousness *and* outward orientation of concern for the well-being of others helps us avoid excessive self-focus such as self-promotion and self-defense—known risk factors for heart disease. Present research also shows a positive relationship between humility and both physical and mental health, especially in reducing stress and increasing social support.[5] This balance of self- and other-concern also lowers risk for being dominated or exploited relationally. It facilitates social and cultural interactions. It develops, maintains, repairs, and restores relationships. And it promotes other positive social behaviors such as:

- Forgiveness
- Faithfulness
- Trust
- Commitment
- Cooperation
- Openness

- Tolerance
- Helpfulness
- Gratitude
- Generosity
- Gentleness

---

5. For more information about this relationship, see Toussaint and Webb, "The Humble Mind and Body," 178–91.

The relationship between humility and one's religion (the adherence to a belief system and practice of an organized religion) or spirituality (a broader feeling of closeness or connection to the sacred) also draws the interest of social scientists. Their research suggests we consolidate various definitions of humility and focus on one common denominator: strongly humble people have less ego involvement than those with less humility. As we will see later in this chapter, all major religions value humility. And as we might expect, researchers find that religious and spiritual people tend to value humility. They see it as a desirable strength and positive attribute. They also are perceived as humble by others, more than their secular or nonreligious counterparts. It may be the case that the prominence of humility in religious teachings does in fact temper self-righteousness, arrogance, and pride in the faithful. In other words, humility grows from faith. Spiritual individuals tend to have more humility and to value forgiveness more than others. Greater humility is associated with feelings of awe toward God. This may be because those grounded in a faith receive more spiritual support, resulting in greater trust in God and a closer relationship with God. In any event, those with high commitment to their faith are perceived as being humbler by others. And contrary to popular belief, research finds that religious people tend to not see themselves as better than others.[6]

Unfortunately, attempts to promote or develop the practice of humility are relatively new endeavors in the social sciences. Psychologists, for example, are beginning to help clients deal with egocentric and self-serving biases. Likewise, psychotherapists are attempting to help people explore their place in the world and to develop realistic self-assessments such as acceptance of their strengths and weaknesses. More will be said about cultivating humility later in this chapter.

Finally, social scientists have yet to explore such topics as the mechanisms for practicing humility, including circumstances where humility may be a liability, the impact of gender and cultural differences, and the role of parents, teachers, partners, and therapists in developing the practice of humility as a positive social behavior and source of human well-being.

---

6. For more information on these findings, see Leach and Ajibade, "Spiritual and Religious Predictors," 192–204.

2. Humility is Contextual.

There is a general sense of humility that includes civility and respect, openness to diversity, bridging differences, and cooperative engagement. But there are also different applications or contexts with unique expressions of accurate assessment, modest portrayal, and other-centeredness. We will consider expressions of humility in five contexts: intellectual, political, religious, cultural, and relational.

Intellectual Humility

Intellectual humility centers on the world of ideas and the ways we acquire, express, and respond to them. It is essential and leads us to treat our ideas accurately. It is open-minded. It leads us to ascribe modest importance to our own ideas as we encounter diverse points of view, listen to their rationales, consider their impacts, and modify our views accordingly. Finally, intellectual humility leads to an other-centeredness that delights in exploring ideas different from our own. It eagerly examines other's perspectives, welcomes learning from others, and appropriately responds to implications of others' ideas.

Political Humility

Political humility impacts how we view and respond to the world of governmental systems and the ways their powers are conceived, organized, and exercised. It strives to accurately understand and appraise the strengths and limitations of the beliefs, assumptions, values, realities, and commitments of their own political system as well as those they encounter.

Also essential is a modest presentation of one's political beliefs, assumptions, values, and practices. Such humility is characterized by openness, civility, and respect rather than being arrogant, off-putting, argumentative, or belligerent. As British politician Vince Cable comments, "Humility in politics means accepting that one party doesn't have all the answers; recognizing that working in partnership is progress not treachery."

Political humility, being other-centered, is attentive to the interpersonal situations, structures, relational commitments, obligations, and nuances of government. It also uses power to serve the common good, rather than ignore the common needs and interests of the governed and instead serve only the interests of those with economic, political, and military power. Observes Jim Yong Kim, South Korean-American physician, anthropologist, and World Bank President: "No matter how good you think you are as a leader, my goodness, the people around you will have all kinds of ideas for how you can get better. So, for me, the most fundamental thing about leadership is to have the humility to continue to get feedback and to try to get better—because your job is to try to help everybody else get better."[7]

In short, as clinical psychologist and professor of psychology Everett L. Worthington Jr. puts it, "Political humility that embodies reflective intrapersonal awareness, modest interpersonal self-presentation, and orientation to building others up is an attitude and social stance that reflects the best of humans and often draws humble reactions from others."[8]

Religious Humility

A review of the collected wisdom about humility from major world religions finds remarkable agreement. Based on the sacred books, teachings, beliefs, and practices of five of the world's major religions—Hinduism, Buddhism, Judaism, Christianity, and Islam—four areas of widespread agreement emerge regarding humility. Each religion:

- Recognizes and appreciates humility and decries its opposite
- Views humility as central and necessary in human life
- Agrees that humility involves an accurate view of self rather than an undue negative assessment of self
- Grounds humility in a transcendent reality that something stands outside of and gives ultimate meaning to the universe[9]

This collective religious wisdom helps identify several practical implications about humility. First, whereas each religion eschews self-aggrandizement, ego-centeredness, and self-importance, a tension can arise if a religion's practice of humility toward others conflicts with humility towards its religious authorities. For example, a religious authority might take a stance that limits the application of humility shown in

---

7. From brainyquote.com.
8. Worthington Jr., "Political Humility," 89.
9. For more information about this review and areas of agreement, see Porter et al., "Religious Perspectives on Humility," 4–61.

a particular case. Thus, "a lack of humility within a religious community is not always hypocritical if the stance is rooted in some other religious principle that recommends a posture other than humility."[10] For instance, the Qur'an instructs Muslim women to dress modestly. Therefore, many Islamic women wear a headscarf to maintain modesty and privacy from unrelated males. While this practice may seem subservient or degrading towards women by outsiders, it is viewed by traditional Muslims as a sign of religious respect and personal security.

Second, each religion has its own formative practices for developing humility. And third, humility in a religious context balances the humble recognition that we are creatures, not the Creator, and a healthy pride in being a special creation of the Creator.[11] Consequently, an accurate religious view of self helps guard against being neither self-aggrandizing nor self-deprecating.

Cultural Humility

Cultural humility evolves in our cross-cultural encounters, engagement, and exchange. Awareness of one's own cultural worldview acknowledges both the limitations of one's own cultural background and experiences as well as the limitations in one's ability to understand others' cultural background and experiences. It also includes placing modest importance on one's own cultural background and experiences. Developing such culturally sensitive and competent skills to navigate our behavior and relationships in today's diverse, cross-cultural, and globally-connected world is essential.

---

10. Porter et al., "Religious Perspectives on Humility," 60.

11. Researchers treat pride as dual-faceted, including authentic pride and hubristic pride. Authentic pride is associated with achievement, competence, expertise, confidence, and healthy self-esteem and functions to create status through prestige. It is linked to positive well-being, mental health, and interpersonal functioning. Hubristic pride is marked by arrogance, conceit, and egotistical self-aggrandizing and functions to create status through dominance. It is linked to chronic anxiety, antisocial misbehaviors, and interpersonal dysfunction. Authentic pride allows for focusing on success and earning power while maintaining a sense of humility, including patterns of agreeableness, conscientiousness, voluntary moral action, and empathy toward out group members. Hubristic pride focuses on control and taking power through superiority, aggression, intimidation, and force, including a sense of grandiosity and entitlement with little empathy or compassion for those who are different from themselves or who get in their way. For more information about pride, see Tracy et al., "Pride: The Fundamental Emotion of Success, Power, and Status," 294–310.

To develop its cultural awareness and sensitivity, one predominately English-speaking congregation reached out to a Spanish-speaking congregation with which it shared its building to schedule a joint worship service. Parts of the service were translated so that everyone could understand what was happening, including the welcome, sermon, and prayers. Other parts of the service were not, particularly parts of worship that were unique to one congregation or the other. For example, while the English-speaking congregation practiced a liturgical-style confession of sin, worship planners decided to invite everyone to come to the front of the sanctuary for spontaneous expressions of confession as was commonplace in the Spanish-speaking congregation. A few English-speaking worshipers remained in their seats and watched while most were willing to try something new even if it was out of their comfort zone. A time for greeting and passing the peace unique to English-speaking worshippers was included even though it felt awkward and created some unease among some Spanish-speaking worshippers. Diverse music was included resulting in a blending of musical styles and language from each congregation. While there was some pushback from worshippers in each congregation afterward, most people in both congregations were very appreciative of the joint worship experience and valued learning to worship in more diverse ways.

Relational Humility

Our assessment of each other's humility significantly affects our interest in pursuing and committing to a relationship. When we are confident that someone has an accurate view of themselves, that they think neither too highly nor too lowly of themselves, that they value others intrinsically as well as themselves, we make a positive assessment of their humility. It gives our relationship potential, particularly if they positively assess our humility. It opens the door to mutuality rather than superiority, to supportiveness rather than defensiveness, to trust rather than insecurity. Relational humility involves "creating a context in which sacrificing for the relationship becomes self-reinforcing because both partners invest heavily and appreciate each other. Thus, investing in the relationship becomes mutually reinforcing, as both partners grow in commitment and both enjoy giving to the relationship. Humility gives relationships the potential to thrive."[12] Relational researchers believe that humility, rather than being a doormat

12. Worthington Jr. et al., "Introduction," 9.

with a sense of interpersonal inferiority, involves "cultivating the kind of relationships in which one is able to transform motivations through viewing oneself as belonging to and committed to something larger than oneself, so that sacrificing for the good of the relationship or collective is tantamount to acting in one's own best interest."[13]

During the joint worship service described above, most worshippers gave up some of their comfort level for the greater good of building better relationships between members of both congregations. The service also reveals the challenge of facing a sense of superiority some worshippers feel about their styles of worship and music. And it shows the way to enhance cultural and relational sensitivity among members of both congregations. In fact, the joint worship service was a transformative experience for many people, increasing their awareness, understanding, appreciation, and experience of people different from themselves.

3. Humility is Beneficial.

"I always say be humble but be firm. Humility and openness are the key to success without compromising your beliefs," says American filmmaker George Hickenlooper. Not surprisingly, the benefits of humility include strengthening social bonds, friendships, supportiveness, mentoring, and workplace collegiality. Humble people are perceived as low maintenance, honest yet sensitive, modest, and other-oriented. We want to be friends with humble people because they are likely to promote our welfare, and we want to be humble to become friends as well. Effects of humility on physical, mental, and spiritual benefits appear to be indirect. For example, humble attitudes and behaviors might help people manage conflicts, thus reducing mental, physical, or spiritual stress.

Humility also is beneficial in buffering our relationships. Thomas Merton, a Trappist monk, writer, theologian, and social activist, offers this wise counsel: "Pride makes us artificial and humility makes us real." Indeed, humility can help prevent relationships from deteriorating due to potentially relationship-harming behaviors such as excessive perfectionism, competitiveness, or moralizing. For example, resentfulness can arise in our relationships with friends when we offer well-intentioned though unwanted moral advice such as this: "I've noticed lately that your drinking seems to be interfering with your work and family life. Have you ever

13. See Davis et al., "Relational Humility," 106.

considered going to AA?" Humility also can repair and strengthen social bonds. Noticing our friend's defensiveness, it is apparent that my expression of care was not appropriate and has strained our relationship. I might follow up with this comment: "I see from your reaction that I'm bugging you about your drinking. Please forgive my judgmental sounding advice. I just care about you and your health." In such instances, humility leads us to look for more appropriate ways to care about our friends.

Another way humility is beneficial is in helping cope with stress and major life transitions. We may find ourselves drowning under unrealistic expectations at work, for example, and must humbly face time constraint limitations and the necessity to adjust our workload stressors to achieve a healthier balance between our lives at work and at home.

Finally, humility is beneficial to societal peace. Research shows that humility promotes pro-environmental attitudes, decreases tendencies to bully and be aggressive, and lessens delinquency and crime. Likewise, humble citizens are more committed to social justice, less combative, and they value diversity. Humility also helps people more fairly evaluate information, manage conflict, and negotiate differences.[14] And, as the editors of the *Handbook of Humility* conclude, "We are walking this life together. We believe that humility will make that walk a more productive, virtuous, and ultimately satisfying experience."[15]

4. Cultivate Humility.

As noted earlier, we know little about how to help people develop or cultivate humility. Fortunately, researchers are increasingly focusing on ways to become humbler persons, partners, leaders, and community members. Early humility intervention research results, though relatively limited, show that gratitude boosts humility, which in turn enables one to feel more grateful. Likewise, empirical research suggests that awe-inspiring experiences through nature, beauty, or great accomplishments, may also create feelings of humility. Awe involves low self-focus, is associated with openness to new information and to broader worldviews, thereby increasing humility. Moreover, self-affirmation boosts humility by reducing defensive

---

14. For more information about these benefits of humility to societal peace, see Worthington Jr. et al., "Epilogue," 352.

15. Worthington Jr. et al., "Epilogue," 354.

biases toward threatening information, enables greater acceptance of one's limitations, and diminishes negative moods.[16]

Promising practical applications from recent research by social psychologists Daryl R. Van Tongeren and David G. Myers suggest six steps to develop humility and to deal with self-oriented motives, cognitive biases, and situational forces that make humility difficult to practice:

- Get feedback from trusted sources to gain an accurate view of ourselves
- Know your tendencies towards biases
- Identify and adjust to situations that challenge you to respond humbly rather than arrogantly
- Since acting humbly requires self-regulation, develop humility through practice
- Practice being humble for its own sake rather than to be rewarded
- Compare ourselves to greatness when we tend to think too highly of ourselves[17]

5. Walk Humbly.

As we learned earlier, humility has important spiritual roots. In the Judeo-Christian tradition, for example, walking humbly centers in trusting a God who is for all of us and partners with us in doing justice and cultivating kindness. Both the Hebrew and Christian traditions focus on the covenant relationship between God and humankind. It is a radical view that God actively engages and partners in bringing wholeness to all humankind, especially liberation from all forms of bondage and freedom from all that enslaves. So, what does the Lord require of humankind? How are we to partner with God and one another in bringing wholeness, liberation, and freedom? In ultimate terms, what is "good"? and, What brings meaning in life?

The Old Testament prophet Micah answers our questions when he says God has shown us what to do: "To do justice, and to love kindness, and to walk humbly with your God" (Mic 6:8). Biblical scholar Philip J.

---

16. For more information on these interventions, see Ruberton et al., "Boosting State Humility," 260–72.

17. Van Tongeren and Myers, "A Social Psychological Perspective," 159-60. Also, I present ways that giving and receiving positive feedback can raise our self-concept to a more accurate level in *Communication in the Church*, 163–64.

King calls this verse the Magna Carta of prophetic religion.[18] These words summarize the teachings of the eighth century BCE prophets, Isaiah, Hosea, and Amos. As Old Testament scholar Bernhard W. Anderson observes, "Here we find, expressed in a single sentence, Amos' demand for justice, Hosea's appeal for the steadfast love that binds people in covenant with God and with one another, and Isaiah's plea for the quiet faith of the humble walk with God."[19]

It is important to grasp the inextricable link between doing justice, loving kindness, and walking humbly. As religious educator Thomas H. Groome urges, "At first reading, it would appear that the first two mandates pertain to our treatment of other people while only the third refers to our relationships with God. In fact . . . all three refer to our relationship with God and all three refer to our relationship with other people. In Yahweh's covenanted community, the measure of one relationship is the measure of the other."[20] Old Testament scholar Walter Brueggemann adds further perspective when he says of these three expectations: "They are not three 'virtues.' They are not three 'things to do.' Rather, they speak of three dimensions of a life of faithfulness, each of which depends on and is reinforced by the other."[21] Ultimately, says Brueggemann, "These may embody all that we need to know in order to be faithful and to be human."[22] In short, the way to walk humbly is to do justice and to love kindness. We will return to this connection in the chapters to follow on showing kindness and doing justice.

6. Humility is Both Caused By
and Cause of Other Practices.

Saint Augustine sees humility as central to other positive social behaviors when he asserts, "Humility is the foundation of all the other virtues; hence, in the soul in which this virtue does not exist there cannot be any other virtue except in mere appearance." American clergyperson James E. Faust adds this thought about the relationship between humility and other practices: "A grateful heart is a beginning of greatness. It is an expression of humility. It

---

18. King, "Micah," 288.
19. Anderson, *Understanding the Old Testament*, 318.
20. Groome, "Walking Humbly With Our God," 47.
21. Brueggemann, "Voices of the Night," 14–15.
22. Brueggemann, "Voices of the Night," 14.

is a foundation for the development of such virtues as prayer, faith, courage, contentment, happiness, love, and well-being."[23]

Humility is linked to greater social relationship functioning and to relationship satisfaction. It increases mutual trust, commitment, and intimacy, thereby deepening and enhancing social bonds. For example, humility at its best is reciprocal because each party in a relationship brings both strengths and weaknesses to it. It places us in a self-initiated, appropriate deferential relationship with another without undermining or limiting our own importance or participation in the relationship as when we allow a colleague to choose where to have lunch. It can, however, be taken advantage of, thus destroying trust and relational health. For example, after deferring to our colleague about where to have lunch, our colleague assumes that they have a green light to spend more time together. Such presumption may lead to resistance on our part if we'd prefer not to develop a closer personal relationship or greater level of intimacy. We can't trust that our relationship is headed in the right direction. This dynamic can even dampen the satisfaction, meaning, and fulfillment we have enjoyed up to now.

Then too, while humility precedes honor, humiliation is a form of embarrassment caused by being disparaged by others or by not living up to our own expectations or standards. We say, for example, "I'm so embarrassed at my behavior that I had to eat humble pie."

Humility also creates and expresses respect for one another. Combined with curiosity and empathy, it facilitates healthy relationships wherein curiosity attracts us to each other, humility creates respect for each other, and empathy generates care for one another's well-being. These three practices are especially helpful when we face difficult conversations, including working through disagreement and conflict with others.[24]

Moreover, humility is a precursor to forgiveness and reconciliation, and leads to extending grace to ourselves and others. If we offend someone by telling an inappropriate or disparaging ethnic joke, the quality of our relationship is likely to take a hit as a climate of unease and awkwardness settles over our conversation. To repair the damage we've done to our reputation and to our relationship, facing our own prejudicial behavior and acknowledging that what we've said is wrong and hurtful will be essential. We may feel regret that we've sullied our reputation for cultural sensitivity and be

---

23. From brainyquote.com.

24. For more information about these three practices, see Stewart, *Personal Communicating and Racial Equity*, 43–57.

sorry that we've created a barrier in our relationship. Indeed, we must face our humiliation and own our wrongdoing both to ourselves and to those we have offended. And to transform and restore our relational health we must humbly admit our offense and ask for forgiveness. We will also need to extend grace and forgiveness to ourselves and hope to receive grace and forgiveness from our conversational partners. Moreover, our relational repair requires repentance—a change in our behavior and assurance that we'll not tell such ethnically insensitive and disparaging jokes in the future.

Finally, humility leads to relational satisfaction because of its contributions to openness, acceptance, growth, and warmth. It fosters openness through self-giving behaviors such as sharing, risking, and assertiveness. It facilitates acceptance by taking the time to listen, build trust, and experience empathy. Growth abounds when we are willing to be supportive, empowering, and curious. And humility creates warmth through genuine caring, authentic connecting, and decision-making mutuality. These four qualities transform our relationships by making them meaningful, satisfying, and fulfilling.[25]

As we will see in coming chapters, humility is related to numerous other positive interpersonal qualities, including gratitude, kindness, generosity, and compassion. Humility also is related to justice, fairness, and mercy.

Summary and Conclusion

The practice of humility is a multi-faceted positive behavior. Findings from research present humility as having an accurate self-assessment, modest self-importance, and appropriate other-centeredness. Humility finds unique expressions across intellectual, political, religious, cultural, and relational contexts. Humility has a variety of benefits, and, while we know relatively little about how to become humbler, some promising best practices are emerging. Walking humbly includes doing justice and cultivating kindness. Humility is related to other practices, many of which will be covered in the chapters to follow. The six guidelines covered in this chapter identify ways humility leads to better relationships, ways that practicing humility has the power to transform relationships for the better in your congregations and everyday lives.

25. I provide further information about how these four qualities are at the heart of relational health in *Communication in the Church*, 122–25.

Practical Applications

1. Which of the three facets of humility most affect the quality of the relationships in your life as well as in your congregation's? Think of examples that have transformed your relationships or could transform them.
2. On a scale of 1-10, 10 being the humblest, where would you place yourself? A significant other? Your faith community?
3. How or in what ways is the three-way love perspective helpful in various arenas of your life and in the life of your congregation?
4. Which findings from humility research do you find most informative and useful? How so?
5. How are the five contexts for practicing humility relevant for you and your congregation, both now and in the future?
6. Which benefits of humility strike you as most important? How so?
7. In what ways do you hope to boost the practice of humility in your relationships? How about for those in your congregation?
8. How does walking humbly relate to your experience and that of your congregation?
9. Which practices related to humility most interest you and why? How about those in your congregation?

For Further Study

Brueggemann, Walter, Sharon Parks, and Thomas H. Groome. *To Act Justly, Love Tenderly, Walk Humbly: An Agenda for Ministers* (Eugene, OR: Wipf & Stock, 1997).

Kirkpatrick, Thomas G. *Communication in the Church: A Handbook for Healthier Relationships* (Lanham, MD: Rowman & Littlefield, 2016).

Lopez, Shane J., and C. R. Snyder, eds. *The Oxford Handbook of Positive Psychology* (New York: Oxford University Press, 2009).

Neafsey, John. *Act Justly, Love Tenderly: Lifelong Lessons in Conscience and Calling* (Maryknoll, NY: Orbis, 2016).

Worthington, Everett L. Jr., Don E. Davis, and Joshua N. Hook, eds. *Handbook of Humility: Theory, Research, and Applications* (New York: Routledge, 2017).

Chapter 2

Experiencing Empathy

Empathy is about finding echoes of another person in yourself.
—Mohsin Hamid

Rejoice with those who rejoice, weep with those who weep.
—Romans 12:15

Pastor Hope's world is shattered when a driver in the next lane of the freeway falls asleep and veers right in front of her. As Hope swerves to avoid a collision, she loses control of her car, careens across two lanes of traffic, slams into the guardrail, and flips over before coming to a stop at the side of the road. Taken to a hospital with severe injuries to her back and legs, surgery is required, followed by pain-filled recovery and rehabilitation.

Hope's partner and a clergy colleague arrive in the waiting room and chat about what to say to Hope when she returns from surgery and begins her recovery. They decide they'll ask Hope what she remembers about the accident and assure her that everything happens for a reason. Maybe she'll come out stronger from her painful recovery and rehab. Understandably unsure of what to say, and well intentioned in their attempt to offer words of comfort, the last thing Hope needs is advice and platitudes. Like Job's "comforters," they just don't get it. Healing and transformation will come, but empathy is what Hope most needs at this time. She needs someone to acknowledge her pain and to be present with her. Hope needs someone to walk alongside her in the grief and despair she'll face in recovery.

This scenario demonstrates how unprepared and unsure we can be in knowing how to help one another face the tragedies we'll all encounter sooner or later in our lives. Yet all too often we offer well-meaning advice and religious platitudes but overlook the power of empathic care and concern to transform our relationships with others in our congregations and everyday lives. Such transformation can help others face overwhelming pain and grief along with the acceptance that healing and recovery will take time. Our relationships in time of crisis can disappoint and fail us even as they have the power to support and sustain us. Here are seven sensible, practical guidelines to learn how empathy can help relationships flourish in our congregations and everyday lives during challenging times, as well as in times of joy and accomplishment. Look for best practices for experiencing empathy that give you the power to transform your relationships for the better.

Guidelines for Experiencing Empathy

1. Think of Empathy as a Multifaceted Process of Sharing, Understanding, and Responding to Others' Experience.

Put simply, empathy is experiencing something of someone else's experience. As we will see, there are various approaches, perspectives, and positions regarding empathy, "from its Germanic origins in theories of art appreciation to its current appearance as an affective state that may play a significant role in morality. Philosophy, psychology, anthropology, and neuroscience are all represented, as are philosophy of mind, aesthetics, ethics, and phenomenology."[1] Typically, though, empathy "is caused by the perceived, imagined, or inferred emotion or plight of another, or it expresses concern for the welfare of another."[2] As such, our experience of empathy normally includes three primary components:

- Sharing
- Understanding
- Responding

Sharing

There is an affective or feeling aspect of empathy involving *sharing* or identifying with another person's subjective experience.[3] It is what the Apostle

---

1. Maibam, "Introduction to Philosophy of Empathy," 1.
2. Maibom, "Introduction: (Almost) Everything You Ever Wanted to Know about Empathy," 2.
3. This sharing or identifying with another person's experience can include a variety

Paul is getting at when he appeals to the Christian community in Rome, "Rejoice with those who rejoice, weep with those who weep." This sharing can include such negative emotions as pain, suffering, distress, or sadness, or such positive emotions as pleasure, joy, relief, or happiness. Here, empathy is seen as a process that includes varying amounts and degrees of feeling *for* or *with* another person, feeling the *same* as they do, and feeling care *for* or *about* another's well-being. For example, remembering what it feels like to be hit in the head by a soccer ball, a coach halts soccer practice to give a comforting hug to a similarly injured player. We may also witness or perceive another's situation, believe or infer that they experience a certain emotion, or imaginatively envision their internal state, frame of mind, or point of view. As Pakistani novelist Mohsin Hamid puts it, "Empathy is about finding echoes of another person in yourself."

Moreover, empathy has become an important part of our emotional intelligence. As best-selling author Daniel H. Pink points out, "What used to matter most were abilities associated with the left side of the brain: linear, sequential, spreadsheet kind of faculties. Those still matter, but they're not enough. What's important now are the characteristics of the brain's right hemisphere: artistry, empathy, inventiveness, big-picture thinking."[4] A word of caution, though: when we experience what others feel or, perhaps, feel our way into another, we may need to sufficiently deal with our own feelings in order to be able to feel for them or feel care about their welfare.[5] For instance, pastor Hope's comforters may have had a similar experience for which painful memories make it difficult to give Hope their full attention.

---

of dimensions, including vicariously entering, catching, matching, sympathizing, experiencing, mirroring, imitating, role playing, being attuned to or resonating with. It is common for researchers to define empathy differently, depending on which dimension they wish to study. For example, a social psychologist interested in the way we empathize with others' feeling of pain may focus on the matching or catching dimension of empathy (sometimes called emotional contagion). Or a philosopher interested in the role of empathy in morality may make a clear distinction between empathy and sympathy while another may treat them the same. With respect to the ways researchers differ in what they mean by empathy, philosophers Amy Coplan and Peter Goldie point out that this multiple use of empathy is a good idea since our everyday use of the term is highly varied and often quite vague. Therefore, they argue, it is not necessary for all researchers to adopt the same meaning (see Coplan and Goldie, "Introduction," xxxi–xxxii).

4. From brainyquote.com.

5. For more information about affective empathy, see Maibom, "Affective Empathy," 22–32.

They may need to take a few moments to set aside their own memories to be emotionally prepared to care about Hope.

Understanding

There is a cognitive or thinking facet of empathy involving *understanding* or "mentalizing" what others experience.[6] For instance, as a Sunday school teacher, I might empathize with a student whom I learn has once again not had breakfast. To explain and predict another's experience, we might theorize or make inferences about what they feel, think, or do from their perspective. We might make a connection between the way our student is easily distracted and the effects of being hungry. Or, we might simulate, imagine, or envision what we would feel, think, or do in their situation. Perhaps we can see ourselves behaving similarly as our student.

Projecting what we would do is efficient and works well when we are like another person. Theorizing about another's perspective is more accurate and time consuming, and works well when we're dissimilar. In either case, we must realize that our own self-interests may skew our understanding of others' perspectives. Such self-interests may include reducing our anxiety, maintaining our self-esteem, or confirming our worldview. This realization may lead us to think we see things as they are, and others are biased. Or, we may seek only information that reduces our anxiety, validates our self-worth, or confirms our pre-existing opinions.[7] Such realization may be necessary in a situation where our strongly held religious views or ethnic stereotypes block or limit our ability, for example, to accurately understand how someone could agree to an arranged marriage. In such instances we'd do well to realize we need to walk in someone else's shoes for a mile before criticizing the person.

Responding

Often, though not always, there is a *responding* component to our experience of empathy. Sometimes there is a behavioral response to empathy wherein

---

6. This understanding of what others experience can include several dimensions, including grasping, theorizing, inferring, knowing what it is like, perspective-taking, imagining, envisioning, simulating, mindreading, and projecting.

7. For more information about cognitive empathy, see Spaulding, "Cognitive Empathy," 13–21.

catching and understanding another's experience motivates us to care about their welfare. For instance, we may share in their good times or help alleviate their concerns. French writer and Buddhist monk, Matthieu Ricard, comments, "Neuroscience has proven that similar areas of the brain are activated both in the person who suffers and in the one who feels empathy. Thus, empathic suffering is a true experience of suffering."[8] Furthermore, recent research is showing that "feeling empathic concern for a person in need does indeed evoke altruistic motivation to see that need relieved."[9] In our opening scenario, had pastor Hope's partner and colleague shared or identified with her pain and understood or grasped her feelings of distress and grief, then perhaps they would be moved to help Hope more by their empathic response than by their words of advice.

Besides sympathy or empathic concern for their distress or sadness, our motivation to care about someone's well-being also may involve such feelings as:

- Warmth
- Joy
- Soft-heartedness
- Tenderness
- Compassion for their relief or happiness

Empathy moves us to engage with other's feelings of sadness or similar emotion when they are negatively affected by their situation—or with feelings of happiness or similar emotion when they are positively affected by what is happening to them. Again, *Rejoice with those who rejoice, and weep with those who weep.*

Yet there can be a tension between *sharing* or *understanding* other's experience and *acting* in response to their experience. Often our understanding is inaccurate and we hesitate to act, getting blamed for lacking empathy. Or we act on inadequate evidence and get it wrong and our empathy goes for naught. Our empathic style can range between the extremes of being large-hearted, hasty, and mistaken, and being careful, cold, or aloof. It helps to remember that our understanding of other's cognitive thoughts and intentions are often more accurate than imagining their affective feelings and desires. One solution to our quandary is to base our empathic

---

8. From brainyquote.com.
9. Batson et al., "Empathy and Altruism," 417, 424.

response to what we think someone is feeling on a rough take on their feelings. And then adjust our response to how they react to our empathic actions. Our reactions might be judged as sympathetic and supportive, or as callous, intrusive, and presumptive.

We might think, for example, that a worship team member is missing yet another planning meeting because they lack commitment. As the team leader we respond with annoyance at their presumedly irresponsible behavior. Then we learn that the leader has taken a new job that makes it impossible for them to attend evening meetings. Our initial annoyance and blaming response transforms into patient understanding and concern for their financial well-being. We even explore re-scheduling future meetings so that everyone can be present. What really matters is getting our reactions right rather than getting the details accurate. Or, as in our worship team example, we can take time to get more information and adjust our empathic sharing, understanding, and actions accordingly. As philosopher Adam Morton puts it, "If you know how somebody thinks they feel, and what they make of somebody else's reactions to what that person thinks they feel, you have at any rate a sense of what their subjective life is like. If we combine this with an assumption that our naïve emotions of fellow feeling are at any rate a starting point for grasping the affect of the other, then the gap between what we are good at imagining and what eludes us is beginning to close."[10]

Then too we are not as good as we should be in our capacity to empathize. As American astrophysicist and science commentator Neil de Grasse Tyson astutely observes, "So maybe part of our formal education should be training in empathy. Imagine how different the world would be if, in fact, that were 'reading, writing, arithmetic, empathy.'"

While our capacity for empathy varies, too little empathy leads to an absence of feeling concern for others. And too much leads to feeling overwhelmed by others' circumstances. Moreover, some circumstances make empathy not always a desirable behavior and we may choose to limit or regulate our empathy. For example, feeling or grasping another's pain may become too painful for us. Or our desire to help may risk being taking advantage of. Or helping others may become too exhausting for us.

---

10. Morton, "Empathy and Imagination," 188. Similarly, psychologists Vivian P. Ta and William Ickes conclude that although we don't have direct access to other people's minds or have perfect knowledge of what they feel and think, our limited knowledge is often "good enough" for successful relationships with them. Moreover, we can often sense when it is best to avoid knowing others' feelings and thoughts if it is apt to cause us pain (see Ta and Ickes, "Empathic Accuracy," 360).

Suppose your congregation decides it would like to become a more diverse, multicultural church. Since your community has affordable housing, refugees are moving into your neighborhood. You congregation begins to reach out to refugee neighbors and genuinely welcomes several immigrant families who begin attending worship services. Everything goes smoothly until one newcomer asks your help as pastor in organizing a nonprofit resettlement support organization. First, you recommend a fund-raiser and grant writer. Then when you learn that the new director has an outstanding arrest warrant for a domestic violence incident, you put them in touch with a pro bono immigration attorney. The attorney soon lets you know that the case is complicated because the arrest warrant is from another state and is best handled by an attorney from that state. You also learn that the presiding judge in the court case requires the accused to return and face charges in person if they are to be reduced or dismissed. After innumerable and increasingly desperate phone calls, you discover that the person is driving without a valid driver's license, has no auto insurance, and has no other means of transportation. You also have reason to believe that funds are not being used appropriately by the resettlement nonprofit's director. At this point, you attempt to limit or regulate your empathy. Eventually, you find yourself emotionally burned out, can think of no other way to be helpful, and tell the person that there is nothing more you can do. After numerous subsequent phone calls, you feel taken advantage of, are empathically exhausted, and decide to take no further calls.

Our experience of empathy can also be biased, self-serving, discriminatory, vary across cultures, and play a questionable role in moral development. More will be said about these limitations later. Finally, we will consider the role that empathy plays in understanding, appreciating, and engaging with art, literature, film, and music.

2. Empathy Plays a Role in the Caring Process.

The process of caring weds the cognitive understanding, affective sharing, and behavioral response components of empathy. It involves:

- Attentiveness and openness to the welfare of others
- Feeling concern for the needs of others
- Being moved to do something to improve the welfare of others

There is a radical dimension to the process of caring. Such caring places special emphasis on considering the context of each person's life, which includes being authentic in our relationships with others and looking beyond stereotypes. And doing so it includes seeing connections between our similarities and differences with others along with expanding the circle of those for whom we care.[11]

Take the case of a person imprisoned for theft. Our understanding of the reasons for this person's plight might reveal that the prisoner was hungry and had no means to obtain food other than to steal an apple from a produce stand. Our transformed understanding also might lead us to imagine what it is like to go hungry and be without access to food. Or we might identify with the prisoner's plight and feel genuine care about the prisoner's well-being. Our new understanding and feeling of concern about the prisoner's vulnerability might motivate us to volunteer at our local food bank. Or get involved with Bread for the World. Or call into question a justice system that punishes another human being for trying to obtain food. Our curiosity might even move us to inquire about the reasons other inmates are in prison and foster a more caring lifestyle going forward. Indeed, empathy plays a large role in caring about the welfare of other people. And it does so both in dire circumstances such as our hungry neighbor experiences as well as in the ordinary circumstances that prevent our lives from flourishing.[12]

Empirical research reveals that empathic understanding and concern also enhance the quality of our social relationships in several important ways, including:

- Greater relationship satisfaction
- Greater popularity
- Lower levels of conflict and aggression
- Higher levels of partner support
- Greater tolerance for partner misbehavior
- Greater willingness to forgive[13]

---

11. For more information about the science of caring, especially in the nursing profession, see Rosa et al., *A Handbook for Caring Science*.

12. For more information about the role of empathy in the caring process, see Hamington, "Empathy and Care Ethics," 264–272.

13. See Davis, "Empathy, Compassion, and Social Relationships," 311.

With respect to instances when partners commit serious wrongdoing, it is the emotional facet of empathy—specifically feelings of compassion—that most contributes to forgiveness. Another important finding from this research is that the influence of empathy on social relationships is consistent across cultures, not just Western cultures.

Here is a summary of empathy's role in social relationships from this research: "For the day-in, day-out maintenance of social relationships—understanding one's partner, offering the proper support, and avoiding the commission of bad behaviors—it is generally the willingness and ability to understand the partner's psychological point of view that is important. However, when relationships are most in jeopardy due to a serious transgression by one of the partners, it is the emotional response of compassion for the offender that largely determines whether or not the offense will be forgiven."[14]

Empathic concern plays a central role in two branches of clinical psychology: Carl Rogers' client-centered psychotherapy, and Heinz Kohut's psychoanalytic self-psychology. Rogers believed that counseling and psychotherapy cannot succeed without a therapist's empathic concern, something he considered difficult to achieve. In fact, "he warned that the therapist must preserve the boundaries between herself and the client, lest she risk over-identifying with the client, which distorts understanding and interferes with the therapeutic process."[15] Like Rogers, Kohut organizes the therapeutic process around empathy, "which he viewed as the most important feature of the psychotherapeutic relationship and values above insight and interpretation."[16]

3. Empathy Plays a Role in Moral Development, Judgment, Motivation, and Responsibility.

The connection between empathy and morality is apparent when we encounter someone who is experiencing pain or distress. While it is common

---

14. Davis, "Empathy, Compassion, and Social Relationships," 311–12.

15. Coplan and Goldie, "Introduction," xix. For more information on empathy in Carl Roger's client-centered counseling and psychotherapy, see Haugh and Merry, *Rogers' Therapeutic Conditions: Evolution, Theory and Practice.*

16. Coplan and Goldie, "Introduction," xix-xx. For more information on the essential place of empathy in the therapeutic process from Heinz Kobut's psychoanalytic perspective, see his publication, *How Does Analysis Cure?*

for us to empathize with other peoples' pain or distress, and even be moved to help alleviate their plight, there remains a question of whether we ought to do so. Our responsibility to illegal immigrants seeing asylum presents such a quandary, as we shall see. When and to what extent are we morally obligated to act? To answer this question, let's examine the relationship between empathy and morality in these four areas:

- Moral development
- Moral judgment
- Moral motivation
- Moral responsibility

Moral Development

The connection between empathy and morality is important in our moral development. Empathy for other people's plight helps develop our sense of right and wrong. Our sense of caring and justice kicks in and informs us that it is right to help someone in need—and, conversely, that it is wrong to ignore or refuse to help them to the extent that we can do so. We develop a moral obligation to act and feel morally guilty if we do not.[17] Take the situation where our country's treatment of illegal immigrants seeking asylum includes separation from their children upon arrest. Even if we support zero tolerance policies for illegal immigrants, our sense of justice may cause us to be critical of such separation practices.

Empathy plays a similar role in our moral judgment, motivation, and responsibility. Our empathic understanding of another's plight and our identification with what they are feeling informs our judgment about whether we ought to help. It also generates our motivation to help, or not. And it identifies the responsibility we do or do not bear. Let's briefly examine these other three areas regarding empathy and morality.

Moral Judgment

With respect to the role of empathy in moral judgment, philosopher and ethicist Antti Kauppinen concludes that "people who lack the ability to

---

17. For more information about the role empathy plays in moral development, see Hoffman, *Empathy and Moral Development*.

put themselves in the place of others and feel for them do appear to have trouble with moral insight and appreciating the grounds of pro-social moral principles, even if their rational powers are largely intact. This suggests that empathy may have an irreplaceable role in the development of good moral judgment."[18] In our immigrant example, citizens whose parents immigrated without fear of persecution may have difficulty empathizing with a desperate illegal immigrant seeking asylum. Or memories of painful separation from loved ones may result in an attack of conscience and lead us to decide we ought to do something to stop such practices or to help reunite separated family members.

Moral Motivation

Philosopher Alison E. Denham suggests that empathy is necessary for moral motivation in countering both indifference and self-interest. She points out that empathy can "provide a powerful motive to right action that sometimes defeats, and often competes with, the two forces most hostile to morality: indifference and self-interest. Empathy competes with indifference in its epistemic role, by alerting us to circumstances that demand moral attention, and in its motivational role, it serves as a corrective to our default position of egocentrically pursuing our own ends, and only our own ends."[19] Indifference to or callous disregard for the plight of people forced to illegally cross a border to pursue their case for asylum may make us turn our backs to their desperation. It may stifle any motivation to care about our government's family separation practices. Or empathy for people in such desperate circumstances may trigger our motivation to protest our country's disregard for the rights of asylum seekers.

Moral Responsibility

"Emotional empathy, suitably understood, does seem necessary for moral responsibility,"[20] asserts philosopher David Shoemaker. But we can get empathy wrong, for several reasons: in-group bias, preferential treatment, and manipulation. However, rather than impugn the role of empathy in moral

18. Kauppinen, "Empathy and Moral Judgment," 225.
19. Denham, "Empathy and Moral Motivation," 228.
20. Shoemaker, "Empathy and Moral Responsibility," 251.

responsibility, such bad things can be eliminated or greatly limited by more empathic concern. As Shoemaker puts it, "It's not that empathy itself is bad or causes bad things; rather, it's the incomplete or improper deployment of empathy that does so. But then we should correct the deployment, not dismiss the empathy."[21] Empathy for persons fearing for their lives may make us sympathetic to their plight but not move us to protest immigration practices that separate families. On the other hand, learning about a neighbor's struggles to navigate our immigration courts may increase our empathy for current asylum seekers. It may even result in reassessing our country's responsibility for helping people as desperate as our neighbors once were—neighbors who now are patriotic and model citizens.

4. Empathy Plays a Role in the Arts.

"The arts enable us to put ourselves in the minds, eyes, ears and hearts of other human beings." So says English film, theater, television, and opera director Sir Richard Eyre. The role of empathy in various art forms, including painting, literature, film, and music, is centered not on what the artist or the object of the artwork understands or feels. Rather, we must understand and feel the perspective or mood of the artist to appreciate or experience the work of *art as intended by the artist*. Artistic empathy is a process of grasping, being attuned to, and seeing the relevance to real life of the object and context of a work of art *as intended by the artist*. Such artistic empathy is required to appreciate or experience the painting of a picture, the language of literature, the production of a film, or the composition of a piece of music. [22]

Even something as commonplace as reading is an exercise in empathy. To follow a novelist's intended character development, for example, it helps to imagine ourselves in the shoes and situations of their characters. Likewise, filmmaking requires empathy. In acting, states American actor and filmmaker Edward Norton, "You're trying to get inside a certain emotional reality or motivational reality and try to figure out what that's about so you can represent it."

---

21. Shoemaker, "Empathy and Moral Responsibility," 247.

22. This emphasis on perspective-taking is a common approach to the role of empathy in the arts found in chapters 25–28 of *The Routledge Handbook of Philosophy of Empathy*: Carroll, "Empathy and Painting," 285–92; Robinson, "Empathy in Music," 293–305; John, "Empathy in Literature," 306–16; and Stadler, "Empathy in Film," 317–26.

Even in wider contexts as diverse as the arts of design and group leadership, empathy is vitally important. For example, Brazilian entrepreneur and Instagram co-founder Mike Krieger says, "Empathy is key in the design process, especially when you start expanding outside of your comfort zone to new languages, cultures, and age groups. If you try to assume what those people want, you're likely to get it wrong."[23] In the same vein, empathy is essential to develop and exhibit the relational qualities required by flexible and adaptable group leaders. For example, the art of effective group leadership requires communication skills such as empathic listening along with empathic concern for member expectations, group morale, and member appreciation.

Finally, in the art of music, consider the challenge facing many congregations in selecting hymns for worship. Empathy for one another's preferred music style (whether traditional, contemporary, or blended) can avoid trust-straining worship wars by creating mutually-agreeable criteria for "good music." For example, if a hymn is musically well written, the content is theologically sound, and it is singer-friendly, then it qualifies as "good music" for use in worship. Such artistic empathy is a way for everyone to appreciate and participate in the singing of hymns as intended by the composers.

5. Empathy is Affected by Individual Differences.

Here are three areas where individual differences may affect our giving or receiving of empathy:

- Gender differences
- Intercultural differences
- Empathy impairment

Gender Differences

Before empirical research began to examine whether gender differences affect our experience of empathy, gender stereotyping or social beliefs about gender and empathy held sway. For example, do mothers really have more empathy than fathers when their child gets injured in a soccer

---

23. From brainyquote.com.

match? What about the common belief that men empathize intellectually while women do so emotionally in their interpersonal relationships? Now, with newer experimental methods and theoretical approaches, research finds no significant gender differences in empathy. As Robyn Bluhm, who examines philosophical issues in neuroscience and medicine, concludes: "With the exception of studies that rely on participants' self-reports, or on others' reports of their behavior, no consistent gender differences in empathy have been observed. This pattern raises the possibility that gender differences in empathy are in the eye of the beholder, and that the beholder is more influenced by gender stereotypes than by empathetic feelings or behaviors themselves."[24]

Intercultural Differences

It often is a daunting task to feel or imagine our way into the lives and experiences of people from cultures different from our own. The accuracy and affects of our empathy can build bridges or create barriers in our intercultural relationships. It can be helpful or hurtful. For instance, what are we to do when neighbors from a different culture raucously celebrate a special ethnic holiday well into the night with no apparent regard for our need to wake up refreshed and go to work early the next morning? Or how are we to problem-solve with our neighbors when their culture handles difficult conversations very differently than we do? Our ability to empathize with intercultural sensitivity often is limited or blocked by anxiety, fear, ignorance, and social context (e.g., culturally, politically, morally, and religiously). Unfortunately, other than the finding that children from collectivistic cultures tend to be better at empathic processes than those from individualistic cultures,[25] empirical research on empathy across cultures has a short history and currently lacks attention by social scientists. Such research to date has not discovered how intercultural empathic processes and their social consequences are experienced, expressed, and evaluated. In fact, researchers studying intercultural relationships "challenge any conception of empathic processes that overemphasizes their innateness, their uniformity, or their moral or political clarity."[26]

---

24. See Bluhm, "Gender and Empathy," 386.
25. See Decety and Meltzoff, "Empathy, Imitation, and the Social Brain," 81.
26. Hollan, "Empathy Across Cultures," 341–52.

Empathy Impairment

Not everyone is equally capable of empathy, however. Those who cannot easily do so, if at all, are psychopaths and those with autism. People with autism typically can feel what things are like for others and be in sync or attuned emotionally. However, they often are lacking or blinded in understanding or imagining other people's mindset. In other words, they have affective empathy but lack cognitive empathy. This helps explain why they can feel for or with others but lack the ability to express or communicate their concern for others. The opposite is true for psychopaths: they have cognitive empathy and lack affective empathy. Unable to feel human distress, they can understand another person's emotional state but are limited or blocked in their ability to resonate with or be attuned to other people. This explains why they typically lack sympathy for others, feel no obligation to help alleviate other people's distress, and feel no remorse when they hurt other people.[27]

6. Empathy Plays A Valuable Role in Society.

"This is a wonderful planet, and it is being completely destroyed by people who have too much money and power and no empathy," observes American novelist Alice Walker. While perhaps overstated, the comment nonetheless illustrates how the experience of empathy is important for our common good. Let's look at five such examples wherein empathy plays a valuable role in society:

- Sports
- Homelessness
- Justice
- Business
- Politics

---

27. For more information about research on empathy and psychopathology, see Kennett, "Empathy and Psychopathology," 364–76.

Sports

As we saw in the introduction of this book, the protest of racial injustice by athletes during the singing of the national anthem is a complicated and many-layered social issue. And the mayor's show of empathy in acknowledging everyone's interests played a valuable role in transforming potentially divisive, out-of-control relationships into a church-sponsored public forum based on mutual respect and understanding. A turn of events in this ongoing public debate occurred when team owners in the National Football League established a new policy to penalize players who do not stand for the national anthem. This new policy sparked another round of public criticism and debate among players, fans, and owners.

The value of empathy, or the lack thereof, in this divisive social issue is illustrated in a radio interview on 710 ESPN Seattle with Doug Baldwin, a then prominent and respected member of the Seattle Seahawks football team. When asked about his work in community advocacy and engagement and his perspective on reaching social justice goals, Baldwin said:

> Honestly I think the biggest takeaway from all the meetings, from all the conversations, from all the research, is there is just a huge lack of empathy within the human race. It really makes me upset. It really disappoints me when I see the things that are going on in our society, the things that are going on in our communities, whether it be mass shootings in schools or harassment between law enforcement and community members, and community members and law enforcement. From the mindset that capitalism infuses into our culture in terms of greed and 'more is better' instead of just being happy with what you have and grateful for what you have. It really upsets me that we don't have more empathy for each other and for the struggles that we all go through.[28]

Indeed, "change begins with understanding and understanding begins by identifying oneself with another person: in a word, empathy," comments Sir Richard Eyre. Recall the touching story of a college softball player, Western Oregon University's Sara Tucholsky, on April 26, 2008, hitting her first home run only to injure her knee rounding first base so severely that she could not finish running the bases on her own power. Stunning their fans and ruining their own chances to advance in the playoffs, the opposing team players, Central Washington University's Mallory Holtman and Liz

---

28. See the 710 ESPN Seattle web post by Rost, "Doug Baldwin: New Anthem Policy Highlights 'Tone-Deafness' Between NFL and Players."

Wallace, carried their injured opponent around the bases so she could score after hitting her three-run homer.[29]

Homelessness

A second social arena wherein empathy plays a valuable role is our ongoing crisis in homelessness. Many city officials and community leaders are attempting to address the causes of homelessness and deal with this vexing social crisis. Seattle University professor Sara Rankin suggests that there is an underlying societal attitude that regards most homeless people as objects to be moved rather than as people to be helped. Here is Rankin's assessment: "It becomes very difficult for people to develop empathy for people who are experiencing this circumstance, and when you can't develop empathy with someone it's really easy to dehumanize them."[30] But, asks Rankin, How many people know someone who is homeless? The need to develop relationships with our homeless neighbors and to experience the kind of empathy that sees them as people needing a place to live is, she suggests, a huge missing link in our search for solutions to the homeless crisis in our society. If so, the power of empathy to transform our relationships with homeless neighbors may significantly impact our social will and motivation to end homelessness.

Fortunately, many congregations and other nonprofit organizations are active in providing overnight housing and support services for homeless neighbors. Consequently, space and opportunity is created to have contact with one another, to get to know one another, and to develop interpersonal relationships that transform strangers into acquaintances for many, and acquaintances into friends for some.

Justice

Our system of justice is a third area of society in which empathy plays a valuable role. For example, in describing his process of making judicial appointments, President Barack Obama says, "We need somebody who's got the heart, the empathy, to recognize what it's like to be a young

---

29. This story is reported in the CBS News web post, "'Unbelievable' Act of Sportsmanship."

30. See The Seattle Times newspaper article by columnist Large, "Laws Pile Up Against Homelessness," B7.

teenage mom, the empathy to understand what it's like to be poor or African American or gay or disabled or old—and that's the criterion by which I'll be selecting my judges."[31] Would that more people involved in our system of justice likewise engage their empathic concern. Such concern is at the heart of adjusting an all-too-common emphasis on punishing people (retributive justice) to include a greater emphasis on transforming people (restorative justice). More will be said in chapter 6 about these two perspectives in our criminal justice system.

Business

Next, we see the value of empathy in the world of business. This comment by American journalist and entrepreneur Ben Parr is particularly salient: "Entrepreneurs may be brutally honest, but fostering relationships with partners and building enduring communities requires empathy, self-sacrifice and a willingness to help others without expecting anything in return." Likewise, it is common for businesses to focus on their bottom line without caring sufficiently about their customer relations. An overemphasis on making a profit and undervaluing the role of empathy in customer relations is often detrimental to a business's success. Indeed, the benefits of empathic listening and the costs of careless listening are immense to business leaders as well as to professionals in fields as diverse as education, medicine, law, and religion.[32]

It is gratifying to see some prominent privileged business leaders feel sufficiently moved by the needs of the less fortunate around the world that they've earmarked a significant portion of their wealth to address major global needs such as health and human services, hunger, poverty, and climate change. Billionaire entrepreneurs such as Bill and Melinda Gates, Michael Bloomberg, and Tom Steyer are notable examples as they model such empathy and commitment to distributive justice.

Politics

Finally, we see empathy playing a valuable role in our political life. Democracy itself, comments former Colorado Governor John Hickenloper, "is

---

31. From brainyquote.com.
32. See Wolff and Marsnik, *Perceptive Listening*, 2–17.

based upon empathy and the recognition that some decisions are solely for the community's benefit without regard to one's own narrow self-interest."

Moreover, with respect to both our national security and our relations with other nations, American lawyer, writer, and presidential advisor Theodore C. Sorensen got it right when he remarks, "We shall listen, not lecture; learn, not threaten. We will enhance our safety by earning the respect of others and showing respect for them. In short, our foreign policy will rest on the traditional American values of restraint and empathy, not on military might."[33]

Similarly, social commentator and pastor John Pavlovitz sees what he calls a "poverty of empathy" in our social and political lives. He believes that too many people do not care about one another. Moreover, he thinks too many political leaders sponsor malicious legislation with callous disregard for the suffering of those needing healthcare, asylum, or a living wage.[34] And yet, seeing a backlash of public opinion to such behavior, he is hopeful: "maybe the outrage so many are expressing today is further proof, that although empathy has died in far too many people, that it is still residing here in the center of our chests, and that this will have to be the thing that propels us into a day and a country that would kill that compassion within us."[35] Perhaps shared trauma such as the global coronavirus pandemic will awaken our empathy for the life and death struggles of so many in the human family.

Congregations and religious institutions are not immune to internal political struggles and stressors. Consider the conservative vs. progressive divide that challenges church governance and shatters peace and unity in congregations and religious bodies. Divisiveness over such moral and theological issues as the welcome and inclusion of LGBTQ+ persons exhausts our energies, splits our religious structures, and depletes our resources. All too often we simply lack sufficient empathy and the capacity to care about finding common ground and rebuilding shattered trust. Elsewhere, I present these eight ways to experience trust by finding common ground:

- Navigate conflicts constructively
- Find unity amid diversity
- Embrace the uncomfortable

---

33. From brainyquote.com.
34. See the web post by Pavlovitrz, "The Death of Empathy."
35. Pavlovitz, "The Death of Empathy."

- Complement rather than oppose
- Use mutual invitation
- Agree on criteria
- Use open space meetings
- Share life-story or faith journeys[36]

7. Empathy Fosters Careful Communication and Creates Healthier Relationships.

Here are four ways that the experience of empathy plays an important role in fostering careful communication and creating healthier relationships:

- Building a supportive communication climate
- Engaging relational communication ethics
- Dealing with differences
- Practicing forgiveness

Building a Supportive Communication Climate

Supportive communication behaviors create healthier relationships than defensive ones. Empathy and indifference are two such contrasting behaviors. Empathy creates a supportive communication climate or positive energy through active listening and openness to ideas different from one's own. By contrast, indifference ignores or refuses to consider another's point of view, thereby creating a climate of defensiveness or negative energy. If our views don't matter, then why continue to talk? Communication requires a commitment to dialogue. So, refusal to be taken seriously is detrimental to relational health—it often creates a hostile climate of defensiveness, resentment, and anger. Those feelings can in turn lead to feeling ignored, isolated, alienated, or estranged. As American-Turkish television personality and cardiothoracic surgeon Mehmet Oz comments, "The opposite of anger is not calmness, its empathy."

---

36. See *Communication in the Church*, 72–77. You'll find examples and practical suggestions for finding common ground and rebuilding trust.

Here's a conversation between two outreach team members that demonstrates the way empathy and indifference affects communication climate and relational health.

Heidi: "You know, Jasmine, that was quite a challenging outreach team meeting last night."

Jasmine: "Well, the conversation was going along nicely until the conflict arose over sponsoring a neighborhood garage sale. Our hearts were surely in the right place."

Heidi: "I'm really glad our congregation feels empathy for the economic well-being of our neighbors. Sponsoring a garage sale was a great way to show we care about our neighbors by giving them an opportunity for some additional income."

Jasmine: "That is, until Jamal blurted out, 'This is a horrible idea!'"

Heidi: "Wow, did that judgmental comment ever stop everyone in their tracks. Talk about throwing cold water on a great idea."

Jasmine: "It surely didn't help matters that Enrique jumped all over Jamal, accusing him of feeling indifferent about the economic challenges of our neighbors."

Heidi: "Yes, Jamal really got defensive until Amos asked him why he thought we shouldn't reach out to our neighbors."

Jasmine: "Jamal did make a crucial point about congregations not being able to legally hold a for-profit activity on church grounds. Too bad he didn't say so earlier before our communication broke down and spiraled out of control with judgmental comments and defensiveness. Thank goodness Amos got our discussion back on track, although it may take some time for Jamal and Enrique to patch up their relationship."

Heidi: "I agree. I'm glad Francine led us out of our quandary by asking, 'What other options do we have for reaching out with care for our neighbors?' I'm glad we came up with some creative alternatives on which we could all agree to pursue at our next meeting."

Notice that empathy for the economic well-being of neighbors is at the center of the outreach team's plan to sponsor a community garage sale. And apparent indifference to those economic challenges sparks the clash between Jamal and Enrique. Fortunately, Amos' inquiry into Enrique's motivation and Francine's conflict management savvy enable the ministry team to get back on track. Unfinished business remains for the relationship between Enrique and Jamal to be repaired and restored.

Engaging Relational Communication Ethics

The field of relational communication ethics is concerned with this question: What are the right, proper, and appropriate communication skills and practices to engage in order to create relational health? Such behaviors include openness, acceptance, growth, and warmth.[37] And empathy, along with listening and trust, guides us in our acceptance of others. Consider a drug addicted youth group member whose family and congregation are perplexed by how they ought to behave toward their troubled teenager. What is the right course of action for them to take? What guidelines can they follow to create effective communication and healthy relationships that will help the teenager find freedom from addiction? Empathy can play a pivotal role in the teenager feeling accepted and in the support community's communication of care and concern. Empathic concern, along with active listening and trust building, are essential best practices. They can help the teenager feel enough acceptance to acknowledge his or her addiction, to share feelings of fear and helplessness, and to express preferences about treatment options. Once a plan to face and treat the addiction is put in place, the caring community will need to guard against allowing their empathy to accommodate or enable resistances to recovery that may tempt the teenager.

Dealing with Differences

Empathy is a useful way to deal constructively with differences we have with others. Treating others the way they would like to be treated, sometimes called platinum empathy, encourages others to stay engaged with us. It helps overcome our typical "flight or fight" mind-set. And it shows poise and confidence in dealing with our differences rather than letting them fester or escalate out of control. Combined with genuine curiosity about others' points of view, and humility that welcomes diversity, platinum empathy creates an atmosphere of cooperation. It leads us to identify

---

37. I present an ethical system based on relational ethics in *Communication in the Church*, 121–25.

the primary issue about which we differ, understand each other's goals, and discover creative alternatives agreeable to everyone. In our conflicts with others, as much as 80 percent of the time, a mutually agreeable, creative, win-win alternative is available if we'll just ask and use the question, "What other options do we have?"[38]

Notice how Amos's curiosity about why Jamal seemed indifferent to neighbors got the outreach team's conversation back on track. It refocused the conversation on the primary goal of caring about the congregation's neighbors. Notice, too, the way Francine's question about other options resulted in fresh alternatives on which the team could agree to pursue at its next meeting.

Empathy also plays an important role in bridging cultural differences. In managing interpersonal conflict in intercultural situations, for example, cultural empathy is an essential communication best practice. According to communication scholars Stella Ting-Toomey and Leeva C. Chung, cultural empathy is "the learned ability of the participants to understand accurately the self-experiences of others from diverse cultures and, concurrently, the ability to convey their understanding responsively and effectively to reach the 'cultural ears' of the culturally different others in the conflict situation."[39] Such understanding was required when neighbors complained about loud music coming from the worship service of a Kenyan fellowship that rented space from a mainline congregation. This clash of cultural sound-level norms between the Kenyan congregation and neighborhood noise ordinances required empathic understanding and careful communication between all parties to arrive at mutually-agreeable solution that restored peaceful church-community relations.

Practicing Forgiveness

Social scientist Everett Worthington Jr. claims that empathy is one of three components for practicing forgiveness, along with humility and commitment. He sees forgiveness as a choice we can make with or without forgetting or pardoning an offense. He believes we can learn to forgive by changing our response from negative emotions such as resentment, hostility, anger, hatred, and vengeance to positive feelings of care, compassion,

---

38. I introduce this point in *Communication in the Church*, 25.
39. Ting-Toomey and Chung, *Understanding Intercultural Communication*, 201.

and conciliation. To help people reach emotional forgiveness he suggests this five-step intervention process:

- Recall the hurt
- Empathize with each other
- Humbly offer the gift of forgiveness
- Commit verbally to forgiveness
- Hold on to forgiveness when remembering past hurts[40]

Taking these steps can transform for the better how we practice forgiveness in our relationships.

Suppose Jamal and Enrique want to repair and restore their relationship following the blow up they created at the outreach team meeting. Using the five steps just identified, their conversation might go something like this:

> **Jamal:** "Say, Enrique, we need to talk. Remember the other night when you jumped all over me for questioning our outreach team's idea of sponsoring a neighborhood garage sale?"
>
> **Enrique:** "Yes, I surely do. What would you like to talk about?"
>
> **Jamal:** "Well, your accusation that I'm indifferent about our neighbors was hurtful to me. You challenged my integrity."
>
> **Enrique:** "How so?"
>
> **Jamal:** "Well you presumed that I don't care about our neighbors. Nothing could be further from the truth. That's why I got defensive."
>
> **Enrique:** "I did learn later that your objection was because churches cannot legally sponsor garage sales. I'm sorry I misinterpreted the reason for your reticence. I guess I'd feel frustrated if someone falsely accused me of something like being indifferent to others. I can understand why you got defensive and feel hurt. I know it is deeply painful when my integrity is threatened."
>
> **Jamal:** "I am glad that you now know why I objected, and that you can understand why falsely accusing me was hurtful. Your empathic understanding is much appreciated."

---

40. For more information about this process and its effectiveness, see Gordon et al., "Forgiveness in Couples," 414–15; and Wade et al., "But Do They Work?," 431.

Enrique: "I now realize I prematurely judged your motives. Please know that I am sorry for jumping to the wrong conclusion. I'm so grateful that Amos asked you why you objected to the garage sale idea. I wish I'd thought to ask you the same question instead of assuming that you were indifferent."

Jamal: "Well, no one is perfect. I could have clarified my objection initially instead of just judgmentally expressing my frustration. Thank you for asking my forgiveness. It will take some time go get over the hurt. I do accept your apology. Knowing that you are sorry will make it easier to heal our relationship."

Enrique: "I'm glad we've been able to talk things out between us and reconcile our differences. I understand that it will take some time to fully restore our relationship. I hope we've all learned anew the importance of checking our perceptions instead of assuming we understand one another. I know I have!"

As we've just seen, empathy plays an important role in the processes of forgiveness and reconciliation. Research finds that victims' reactions to wrongdoing "tend to be harsher, more vengeful, and more hostile if they have negative reactions such as low empathy, low tolerance for misbehavior, high self-restraint, and external motivation. Conversely, victims' powerful impulse toward vengeance is tempered and greater forgiveness occurs when they tend to have such positive reactions as empathy, insight and understanding, agreeableness, and tolerance of misbehavior."[41]

Research also finds that gut-level impulses tend to be hostile and vengeful immediately following the perception of wrongdoing. These impulses vary according to the severity of wrongdoing, the nature of empathy, and the level of commitment. For example, complete forgiveness over time is enhanced by empathy and commitment more than from severity of wrongdoing or degree of restraint and forbearance.

Reconciliation, relational repair, and ongoing relational health are likewise enhanced by victim restraint, forbearance, and extended forgiveness. Empathetic listening to the wrongdoer's perception of wrongdoing and its consequences is an especially important skill to practice. Also important is accepting the wrongdoer's apology and promises that the wrongdoing won't be repeated, as well as the wrongdoer making amends. Finally, in cases of parental neglect, sexual abuse, or domestic violence, if the goal is to facilitate victim healing, then forgiveness can be one way to reduce anger and increase empathy. It is important to note, however:

---

41. *Communication in the Church*, 92.

If healing also includes victim safety, then forgiveness may be a secondary concern and stay in the background until a victim requests help with forgiveness. Otherwise, efforts to facilitate forgiveness may be unhelpful, offensive, and compound unsafe feelings. And in no cases must forgiveness be used to excuse an offender or to forget or trivialize an offense. Such coercive efforts further victimize the victim. When victims do desire forgiveness, most likely they will need an apology and seek remorse from their offender. They will also need a safe place for dialogue to occur.[42]

Summary and Conclusion

Empathy centers on experiencing something of someone else's experience. It includes a multifaceted process of sharing, understanding, and responding to others' experiences. While our understanding of others' experiences is often inaccurate or based on inadequate evidence, what matters most is getting our reactions right. We may need to get more information and adjust our empathic sharing, understanding, and actions accordingly.

The process of caring includes understanding the welfare of others, feeling concern for their needs, and being moved to improve their well-being. Whether in dire or ordinary circumstances, our empathic concern seeks to enable all lives to flourish and grow.

We examined the relationship between empathy and morality, including the role empathy plays in moral development, judgment, motivation, and responsibility. We also saw that empathy enables us to understand how artists intend us to appreciate and respond to their paintings, literature, films, and music.

With respect to ways individual differences affect our experience of empathy we discovered few gender differences. We also found challenging intercultural differences along with impairment of empathy for those with autism and for psychopaths.

Next, we learned that empathy plays a valuable role in transforming our social lives, including the areas of sports, homelessness, justice, business, and politics. And, finally, we saw that empathy transforms our relationships by creating supportive communication climates, engaging relational communication ethics, enabling us to deal with differences, and helping us practice forgiveness.

---

42. *Communication in the Church*, 112.

The seven guidelines presented in this chapter show how our experience of empathy has the power to transform our relationships for the better in our congregations and everyday lives.

Practical Applications

1. Think of a time in your life when you or your congregation experienced a crisis, a difficult challenge, or a major accomplishment. How did people close to you or in your congregation express their empathy, if at all? How would you have liked them to do so?
2. How good are you and members of your congregation at "finding echoes of another person in yourselves?" How or in what ways can you and members of your congregation improve your empathic understanding, sharing, and responding?
3. How have you and your congregation handled situations when experiencing empathy was challenging or even inappropriate? How would you and your congregation limit or regulate the experience of empathy differently in the future?
4. In what ways has empathy played a role in your or your congregation's appreciation of or participation in the arts?
5. How has empathy been a factor in building bridges or creating barriers in your and your congregation's relationships with people from cultures different from your own?
6. What value do you see for the role of empathy in such social areas as sports, homelessness, justice, business, and politics?
7. In what ways have you seen empathy foster careful communication or create healthier relationships in your congregation and everyday life?

For Further Study

Coplan, Amy, and Peter Goldie. *Empathy: Philosophical and Psychological Perspectives* (New York: Oxford University Press, 2014).
Haugh, Sheila, and Tony Merry, eds. *Rogers' Therapeutic Conditions: Evolution, Theory and Practice*, Vol. 2: *Empathy* (Monmouth, UK: 2001).
Hoffman, Martin L. *Empathy and Moral Development: Implications for Caring and Justice* (New York: Cambridge University Press, 2001).
Maibam, Heidi L, ed. *Empathy and Morality* (New York: Oxford University Press, 2014).
———. *The Routledge Handbook of Philosophy of Empathy* (New York: Routledge, 2017).

Chapter 3

Feeling Compassion

*When Jesus saw the crowds, he had compassion for them,
because they were harassed and helpless.*—Matthew 9:36

*I truly believe that compassion provides the basis
for human survival.*—Dalai Lama

As members of a congregation's sharing and support group settle into comfortable chairs and finish their greetings and chitchat, their conversation gets more personal.

"Did you hear about Janie?" asks Hal.

"No," responds Seymour. "I wondered why she isn't here tonight. I just saw Janie at her 39th birthday celebration over the weekend. We all partied pretty hard, but everyone left in good spirits."

"Well, I got a call from her mom this morning telling me that Janie almost died last night and is in the ICU," says Hal.

To which Seymour exclaims, "Wow. What happened?"

Hal then explains, "Apparently Janie thought she came down with the flu over the weekend. According to her mom, she wasn't getting better on Monday or Tuesday, and didn't realize that her diabetes was way out of control. She was tired, didn't feel like eating, and had a fever. She felt really miserable."

"Well, I can see why. She did some serious drinking at her birthday party. We all did, by the way," acknowledges Seymour.

Continues Hal, "By Tuesday evening she began having difficulty breathing, and then when she felt chest pains, she asked her son to call 911. I just visited Janie in the hospital a little while ago, and she told me that her blood sugar count was sky high when she got to the emergency room. By this morning, it was still way too high, and the ICU doctors are trying to get it back under control. She was told she could easily have suffered cardiac arrest had her son not called 911 when he did. I'm really concerned about Janie's well-being. I feel for her and hope she recovers quickly without any more complications."

Reflects Seymour, "Well, I can just hear some of Janie's colleagues at work, perhaps even some people in the congregation, saying that they don't feel very sorry for her. They'll think her pain and suffering are really her own fault. After all, if a type-1 diabetic drinks that much and doesn't take better care of themselves, that's what can happen to any of us. 'Serves her right,' some will say. I guess they do have a point. Maybe her close call with death will make her take a lot better care of herself when she turns 40 next year. Maybe it will make us all stop and think about our drinking behavior."

This scenario demonstrates how our response to someone's pain and suffering can vary—from feeling compassion to feeling disgust, from empathic understanding to ethical judgments about someone's irresponsible behavior. When we perceive that people are responsible for their own misery, it is tempting to feel little compassion or, perhaps more likely, to feel little desire to help alleviate their pain and suffering. It is understandable that people who think Janie's challenging medical situation is self-inflicted will appropriately respond with unsympathetic feelings of anger, blame, annoyance, callousness, or avoidance. Others, though, will respond with compassionate feelings of empathic resonance, personal identification, heartfelt concern, and a desire to help her face challenging circumstances regardless of the cause of her suffering.

But what leads us to feel compassion for some people and not for others? Or to feel compassion some of the time for some people, rather than anytime anyone's well-being is threatened by challenging circumstances? After all, don't we all face serious troubles that threaten our welfare from time to time? And don't we all hope people will feel enough compassion for us that they will be motivated to show their heartfelt concern in compassionate actions to help restore our well-being? In this chapter, you'll find seven guidelines of practical wisdom to learn how compassion offers us better ways for our relationships to flourish during times of crises, as well as in the normal challenges we face in our lives. Also, look for best practices gleaned from recent research for feeling and showing compassion that gives us the power to transform our relationships for the better in our congregations and everyday lives.

Guidelines for Feeling Compassion

1. Think of Compassion as a Heart-felt Feeling of Concern about Challenging Circumstances That Threaten Someone's Well-being, Often Resulting in a Desire to Show Our Care in Concrete Actions That Help Them Face Such Challenges.

Defining Compassion

Often we think of "showing" compassion to someone who is suffering or in pain.[1] However, showing compassion is an action that may follow from knowing someone is deeply troubled and from a feeling of compassion about their resultant pain, suffering, or unmet need. Compassion literally means "to suffer with." At its most basic level, then, compassion is a heart-felt feeling of concern about challenging circumstances that threaten someone's well-being. It is a gut-level feeling that touches us deeply. In Buddhism, according to the Dalai Lama, "Compassion is defined as the wish that all beings be free of their suffering."[2] Or, as Lord Byron observes, *the dew of compassion is a tear*. This deeply felt concern for someone's welfare often results in a desire to show our concern or a caregiving motivation to help them face their threatening circumstances.

Professor of public health and medicine Eric J. Cassell says: "From the time of Aristotle, compassion has been defined as an emotion experienced when individuals witness another person suffering through serious troubles, which are not self-inflicted and that we can picture ourselves experiencing. Compassion at its core is, therefore, a process of connecting by identifying with another person. The identification with others generated from compassion can then provide the motivation to do something to

---

1. One of the valuable lessons of Buddhism is the difference between pain and suffering. As clinical psychologist Louis Cozolino points out in *The Neuroscience of Psychotherapy*, 433, pain is an inevitable part of life that we experience with aging, loss, and death, whereas suffering is the anguish we feel from worry about the future or regret about what has or has not happened in our past. Shame, he points out, is a primary cause of suffering. It is relentless in making us feel badly about our thoughts, feelings, or behaviors. To alleviate suffering, Cozolino suggests mastering three agents of change: come to grips with past trauma, take on the risks of connecting with others, and turn our minds into our allies. It will be helpful to keep these distinctions and suggestions in mind as this chapter unfolds.

2. The Dalai Lama, *An Open Heart*, ix. Also see the Dalai Lama, *How to Be Compassionate*, 78 and 84, wherein he points out that we all want happiness and not suffering, and that the only way to achieve happiness is through compassion for the welfare of all humanity.

relieve the suffering of others."³ This definition makes clear why people's negative reaction to Janie's irresponsible behavior is an understandable and appropriate response. If we can picture ourselves in the same situation, though, our self-identification with Janie's plight makes our compassionate response understandable and appropriate.

Social science researchers Jennifer L. Goetz and Emiliana Simon-Thomas offer a similar working definition of compassion as an emotional experience. For them, "compassion is conceived as a state of concern for the suffering or unmet need of another, coupled with a desire to alleviate that suffering."⁴ Their definition of compassion includes the following distinct components:

- Awareness of an antecedent (i.e., suffering or need in another individual)
- Feeling "moved"; that is, having a subjective physical experience that often involves involuntary arousal of branches of the autonomic nervous system
- Appraisal of one's own bodily feeling, social role, and abilities within the context of the suffering
- Judgments about the person who is suffering and the situational context
- Engagement of the neural systems that drive social affiliation and caregiving, and motivate helping⁵

In short, compassion has a cognitive dimension—noticing another's pain or suffering, an affective dimension—feeling deep concern for the person's pain or suffering, and a behavioral dimension—acting to ease the pain or suffering.

Experiencing Compassion

Let's examine several features of our experience of compassion as the feeling aroused by an awareness of someone's trouble, suffering, or pain.⁶ Our

---

3. Cassell, "Compassion," 393.
4. Goetz and Simon-Thomas, "The Landscape of Compassion," 3.
5. Goetz and Simon-Thomas, "The Landscape of Compassion," 3.
6. It should be noted that some researchers approach compassion differently than as a discrete emotion. For example, some define compassion as a cultivated attitude, others

connection with people's challenging circumstances requires knowledge that their well-being is threatened. Because the experience and response to difficulties and suffering is highly personal and unique to each person, our awareness of others' serious troubles may require a variety of methods of detection, including:

- Identification with the sufferer
- Knowledge of suffering behaviors
- Sights and sounds of suffering
- Transfer of feelings
- Change in goals and purposes of sufferers
- Absence of the sufferer from a group[7]

Generally, compassion evokes a caregiving motivation or desire to do something to relieve a person's pain, suffering or unmet need—to show compassion. So while the wish to be helpful is not in itself compassion, our emotion of compassion may motivate behavior that reduces the tension brought about by the emotion. However, our ability to connect and identify with a troubled and suffering person varies in degree, magnitude, or intensity according to the person and the circumstances. For example, as evident in our opening scenario, self-inflicted suffering by a stranger may evoke little desire to show compassion while we may rush to the hospital out of deep concern for a friend we've just learned is an accident victim and in critical condition following surgery[8]. Even though Janie's problems are self-inflicted, our friendship overrides that reality and we visit her in the hospital and show compassion anyway. We still care about her, even though her woes are self-inflicted.

---

as a trait-like disposition, and still others as a core motivation. For more information about the validity and contribution of these various approaches to thinking about compassion, see Goetz and Simon-Thomas, "The Landscape of Compassion," 4–6.

7. Cassell, "Compassion," 400.

8. For more information about compassion for strangers, see Ekman and Ekman, "Is Global Compassion Achievable?," 41–49. These researchers hypothesize that stranger compassion—what they call global compassion (concern to alleviate the suffering of anyone, regardless of their culture, nationality, language, or religion)— is active from early life in some, but not most, people without some event activating it. Further research is needed to determine if this activation event or cultivation of compassion occurs from mere chance, upbringing, genetic factors, training, life experiences, or environmental circumstances.

Other factors may affect our motivation, desire, and willingness to show compassion even after we've initially felt moved by someone's situation. Exposure to suffering doesn't necessarily result in feeling compassion. Such exposure might lead us to feel personal distress, indifference, annoyance, being overwhelmed, satisfaction, or even anger. For example, we might be upset more *by* someone's suffering than *for* their suffering. Sometimes referred to as compassion fatigue or empathic distress fatigue, it may interfere with compassion by making compassion difficult to tolerate or even frightening. We can also lose sight of the boundary between ourselves and the troubled person. Consequently, we may need to deal with or transcend our personal distress or fatigue before we can take compassionate actions.

We may also feel indifferent to someone's suffering because we fail to notice it or decide to not show compassion. Or we may decide to suppress our feelings of compassion or reassess the circumstances, leading us to feel annoyance or callousness. It should not be a surprise that there are parishioners who have some of these feelings about Janie, perhaps even some of her small group members.

Then too, when someone's well-being appears unlikely to get better or their challenging circumstances seem overwhelming, even with our intervention, we may take the perspective of a bystander who decides not to become involved. Moreover, there may be times when we take pleasure or satisfaction in others' suffering if we think the person deserves it. For example, we may assess the suffering person's behavior as despicable, overly self-serving, deserving of punishment, or unethical. And finally, we may feel disgust or anger at the causes of someone's suffering if we judge them as unfair or unjust, as with victims of domestic violence or children injured in war. Our own exposure to dangerous or threatening situations, or our feelings of inadequacy in our capacity to help, may also affect our feelings of compassion. They may cause us to reappraise, block, regulate, or limit our care giving motivation and behavior.[9]

As we have just seen, depending on how we assess ourselves, the suffering, and the context, our experience of compassion includes positive as well as negative emotions. We may have negative feelings about certain aspects of

---

9. Results from evolutionary and neurobiology research of compassion indicate that there may be gender differences in compassion. For example, Carter et al. in "The Roots of Compassion," 181, report that females in general may be more capable than men of appreciating the suffering of others, while men may have greater variation in the capacity for compassion.

the situation, the suffering person's circumstances, or our own involvement. Or we may have positive feelings about our motivation to help, our compassionate actions, the relief we see in someone's suffering, or the removal of threats to their welfare. For instance, we may experience a displeasing impatience or intolerance for suffering or have a welcoming empathic sensitivity or joy from helping. In short, whereas compassion is typically viewed as a positive emotion, it may be experienced both pleasantly and unpleasantly, as we've seen in the above situations and examples.[10]

2. Our Brains Are Wired to Thrive on Compassion.

Our brains are built to depend on compassion and other related pro-social feelings, thoughts, and behaviors for our well-being. The Dalai Lama says, "I truly believe that compassion provides the basis of human survival." Clinical psychologist Paul Gilbert points out that "our brains have evolved *to be caring* and *to need caring* to such an extent that the way they shape and wire themselves throughout life, the pattern of their interconnections, is significantly influenced by the affection, love and caring they receive.... This is the way our brains are built. We depend on care and love."[11] Gilbert goes on to explain:

> Children (and adults) who receive kindness, gentleness, warmth and compassion are, compared with those who don't, more confident and secure, happier and less vulnerable to mental and

---

10. Results from cross-cultural research are finding important similarities and differences about how people from different cultures understand, experience, and express compassion. For example, while people across cultures view compassion as emotional, Western cultures feel the most compassion for those with whom they can identify, feel like, and share perspectives. Buddhist views of compassion, in contrast, assume that since everyone and everything is interconnected, people should feel compassion towards everyone, including adversaries and wrongdoers. Moreover, distinctions between the cognitive and emotional aspects of compassion may vary among cultures. Furthermore, some cultures value spontaneous acts of compassion more than reciprocal ones while others value both types of motivation. And people from poorer nations are more likely to feel and express compassion than those from wealthier nations. Finally, some cultures tend to focus on positive aspects of compassion while others focus on the negative. For instance, Americans tend to send sympathy cards emphasizing good memories while Germans more often send cards centered on people's loss and sadness. For more information on ways culture shapes compassion, see Koopmann-Holm and Tsai, "The Cultural Shaping of Compassion," 273–85.

11. Gilbert, *The Compassionate Mind*, 49–50. Also see Cozolino, *The Neuroscience of Human Relationships*.

physical health problems; they are also more caring and respectful of others. Receiving kindness, gentleness, warmth and compassion tells the brain that the world is safe and other people are helpful rather than harmful. Receiving kindness, gentleness, warmth and compassion improves our immune system and reduces the levels of stress hormones. Receiving kindness, gentleness, warmth and compassion helps us to feel soothed and settled and is conducive to good sleep. Kindness, gentleness, warmth and compassion are like basic vitamins for our minds.[12]

For instance, when we show compassion to ourselves by having patience with challenges at work, our brains send signals to our central nervous systems that allow us to relax, reduce our level of stress, and enjoy our work. We can override anxiety, think more clearly, and face challenges with courage. It is also why victims of domestic abuse experience fear, humiliation, and anger—that's the way our brains are wired. Or when we put our arms around a grieving neighbor who has just lost a parent to cancer, they feel care and comfort. Our nonverbal communication signals our neighbor's brain to trigger their human soothing and contentment system,[13] such that they experience affection, appreciation, and support.

Not only are our brains wired to need caring from others, so too our human relationships have the power to shape and reshape our brains throughout our lives. "It is the power of being with others that shapes our brains,"[14] asserts clinical psychologist Louis Cozolino. Gilbert puts it this way: "Positive social relationships not only provide individuals who will look after you if you're sick, but they can have an impact on your immune system, too. Today some economists use the term 'social capital' to describe the benefits we gain from our mutual supportiveness and connectedness, but it is useful to keep in mind the physiological benefits of supportive, interconnected relationships, too. Such relationships also have a major impact on the soothing/contentment system."[15] Compassion arises from balancing the clusters of neurons in our soothing and contentment system with those in our threat and self-protection system and our incentive and resource-seeking system.

12. Gilbert, *The Compassionate Mind*, 49-50.
13. Gilbert discusses this emotional regulation system along with its two counterparts, our threat and self-protection system and our incentive and resource-seeking system, in *The Compassionate Mind*, chapters 2-5.
14. Cozolino, *The Neuroscience of Human Relationships*, xix.
15. Paul Gilbert, *The Compassionate Mind*, 54.

Indeed, *our brains shape our relationships even as our relationships shape our brains.* Cozolino points out, for example, that the transformative power of intimacy is rooted in the evolution and development of the brain through parenting, friendship, and love—the same power used in psychotherapy, education, and ministry.[16] And commenting more broadly about the power of loving relationships to shape our brains, Cozolino says this: "Loving relationships help our brains to develop, integrate, and remain flexible. Through love we regulate each other's brain chemistry, sense of well-being, and immunological functioning. And when the drive to love is thwarted—when we are frightened, abused, or neglected—our mental health is compromised."[17]

As we'll see in the next section, on developing our capacity for compassion, this connection between our social brains and compassion is why much compassion training is mind-based. In fact, compassionate mind training deliberately fosters these brain patterns. As Gilbert puts it:

> When we're in kind relationships rather than critical ones, the levels of our stress hormones are lower and our feel-good brain chemicals higher and our immune systems are more robust. The same is true when we treat *ourselves* with compassion rather than criticism. Compassion is also a major pattern generator in our brains—it harnesses certain motives and competencies and organizes them in certain ways, ways that are very conducive to our minds' and bodies' experience of well-being. But we need to focus and train the brain to develop our compassion abilities to reap these rewards.[18]

3. Feel and Practice Self-Compassion.

Thus far, when considering someone's suffering, we've focused on other people's suffering. But what happens when the person suffering is us? Are we dependent only on the help of others to find relief? Surely self-compassion can cause or be caused by narcissism, selfishness, self-indulgence, laziness, or weakness. However, there is a healthy type of compassion we may have for ourselves. Self-compassion takes the perspective of the compassionate other towards us and helps put our situation in context.

---

16. Cozolino, *The Neuroscience of Human Relationships*, 12.
17. Cozolino, *The Neuroscience of Human Relationships*, 399.
18. Gilbert, *The Compassionate Mind*, 216.

We can remember that everyone suffers. We can be kind to ourselves. And we can be mindful about replacing unhealthy feelings, thoughts, and behaviors with healthy ones. Let's more closely examine these three components of feeling and practicing self-compassion, as well as consider the benefits of self-compassion.

We All Suffer

Often we relate to our own suffering as though our experience is unique and unrelated to that of others. We lose sight of the fact that *we all suffer*. Moreover, we're all works-in-progress. Everyone has shortcomings, makes mistakes, fails, and misbehaves. Even when our misery happens through no fault of our own, we can feel isolated or cut off from others. It helps to remember that we are not alone in our suffering and shortcomings—misery is part of our common or shared humanity.

Self-Kindness

We also can assume others are having an easier time with their suffering and that our situation is abnormal or unfair. We often may beat ourselves up rather than be patient with and supportive of ourselves. Even when our plight is beyond our control, such as a traumatic or accidental event, we can so focus on solving our problems that we ignore being comforting, sympathetic, calming, and kind to ourselves. For example, we may get so bogged down in worry and self-doubt over losing our job that we fail to remember that our termination was not our fault, and that we still have very marketable skills. Being kind to ourselves also acknowledges our flaws rather than being overly critical of our mistakes and failures. As psychologists Kristin Neff and Christopher Germer put it:

> [Self-kindness] entails relating to our mistakes and failings with tolerance and understanding and recognizing that perfection is unattainable. Self-compassion is expressed in internal dialogues that are benevolent and encouraging rather than cruel or disparaging. Instead of berating ourselves for being inadequate, we offer ourselves warmth and unconditional acceptance. Instead of getting fixated in a problem-solving mode and ignoring our own suffering, we pause to emotionally comfort ourselves when confronting painful situations. With self-kindness we make a peace

offering of warmth, gentleness, and sympathy from ourselves to ourselves so that true healing can occur.[19]

Practice Mindfulness

Besides realizing that our life challenges and our personal failures are not unique, and being kind to ourselves, we can use the practice of *mindfulness* to not allow such feelings, thinking, and behaviors to enter our awareness as:

- Avoidance or denial
- Exaggerated failure or disappointment
- Harsh judgment
- Obsessive self-pity
- Dysfunctional coping strategies
- Unkind self-care

Mindfulness helps us take the perspective of the "compassionate other" toward ourselves. It acknowledges rather than ignores or suppresses our struggles and pain, and it helps put our situation in context. Mindful that our suffering and shortcomings are shared with all humanity, we can feel less isolated, think about our unpleasant situations with nonjudgmental understanding and non-defensive acceptance, and treat ourselves with wise strategies of proper concern, care, support, and kindness.

Benefits of Self-Compassion

Early empirical research finds a wide array of links between self-compassion and intrapersonal and interpersonal well-being, including such benefits as:

- Increased happiness, curiosity, motivation, competence, and social connectedness
- Decreased depression, stress, anxiety, negativity, fear of failure, and extreme reactions
- More accepting thoughts, putting problems in perspective, and taking responsibility

---

19. Neff and Germer, "Self-Compassion and Psychological Well-being," 372.

- Acknowledging and validating the importance of both positive and negative emotions[20]

These benefits of self-compassion illustrate what can happen when we treat ourselves with inner kindness rather than inner neglect. We become our own best ally rather than our own worst enemy. Neff and Germer aptly conclude, "When we are mindful of our suffering and respond to it with kindness, remembering that suffering is part of the shared human condition, it appears that we are able to better cope with life's struggles."[21]

Likewise, Paul Gilbert concurs that "the evidence is now overwhelming: feeling love and compassion for ourselves and others is deeply healing and soothing, and helps us face the many challenges that will come our way."[22] In fact, Gilbert points out that finding happiness is a benefit of compassion—and so much more:

> It can help us to cope with failure, to take risks, to practice and deal with our failures on the path to competence, to deal with criticism and conflicts, to develop more harmonious relationships. It can become a focus for our self-identity, something to strive for and work at. It can help us to link to a caring/soothing aspect of our mind, and to face and cope with life's tragedies. In recognizing that we live in a sea of suffering, we can find meaning and purpose if we dedicate ourselves to bringing compassion into the world. And it can help us to develop wisdom so that we can step back from vengeful, fearful and aggressive solutions to problems and seek instead fairness, justice and kindness for all of us in a world of limited resources.[23]

4. Organizations Can Be Compassionate.

Just as there are compassionate individuals, so also are there compassionate organizations. Compassionate responses to pain and suffering can be part of an organization's culture. For example, Janie's sharing and support group members may decide to take compassionate actions such as

---

20. Neff and Germer, "Self-Compassion and Psychological Well-being," 373-75. Most findings from these studies are based on correlational data and research is on-going to determine causes for the links between self-compassion and well-being.

21. Neff and Germer, "Self-Compassion and Psychological Well-being," 382.

22. Gilbert, *The Compassionate Mind*, xxii.

23. Gilbert, *The Compassionate Mind*, 215.

preparing meals for her during her recovery. Likewise, Janie's supervisor or CEO might demonstrate her work organization's culture and climate of compassion by offering her extended paid sick leave or helping with unexpected medical bills.

Research finds that such collective compassion improves organizational performance. For instance, it buffers organizations from negative effects of trauma and distress. It also increases resilience and recovery from the pain and suffering caused by employee misfortune or created in organizations.[24]

While research on the impact of leaders on compassion in organizations is still in its early stages, possible ways leaders can use their power and influence to draw out compassion in an organization include:

- Creating a climate where suffering is noticed, legitimized, expressed, and supported
- Directing attention of others to suffering and its alleviation
- Encouraging and modeling expressions of empathic concern, care, and affection
- Being a catalyst for mobilizing an array of resources to alleviate suffering[25]

Further research is needed to understand how organizations can enable more compassion, deal with compassion fatigue, and take culturally appropriate compassionate actions. We may also need to learn how to express compassion in combination with other positive social behaviors such as kindness, generosity, and love.[26]

5. Manage Compassion Stress and Fatigue.

Earlier we learned that even though compassion is beneficial, our experience of compassion can result in high levels of stress and fatigue. But what inhibits compassion in the first place? And what are the causes or predictors of compassion stress and fatigue along with possible prevention and coping

---

24. Cameron, "Organizational Compassion," 425–30.

25. Worline and Dutton, "How Leaders Shape Compassion Processes in Organizations," 439–53.

26. Cameron, "Organizational Compassion," 430–31.

mechanisms? Let's examine possible compassion inhibitors, and particular risk and protection factors to reduce compassion stress and fatigue.

Compassion Inhibitors

Before considering ways to reduce compassion stress and fatigue, it is helpful to understand what inhibits compassion in the first place. First, there are role-linked conditions that inhibit compassion such as when caring is obligatory or when other's needs are greater than available resources or what we want to devote to caring. In addition, stress can arise when we're uncertain or unclear about what to do, or when we lack necessary support. For example, we may feel trapped in a caring role for a family member with dementia or mental illness, creating conflict between wanting to care and resenting limitations to our lifestyle—and then feeling shame and guilt about our resentment. Other strains in the caring role that lead to compassion stress and fatigue include:

- Weariness or burnout (e.g., no one to relieve us)
- Financial limitations
- Sadness or grief about losing the person we once knew
- Difficulty coping with aggressive behavior, unreasonable demands, or changes in physical or mental capacities of the one for whom we're caring
- Feeling inadequate about our caring

Next, there are contextual factors that can inhibit compassion, including:

- Care-giving staff inadequacies, turnover, or shortages
- Limited caring time
- Lack of caring options when something goes wrong
- Caring system bureaucracy
- Frequent institutional management reorganization
- Uncertainties about the future

Such inhibitors to compassion are especially apparent in our caring roles for those in long-term hospitalization, dementia care facilities, nursing homes, and acute psychiatric units.

Fears, blocks, and resistance also inhibit compassion and can result in stress and fatigue. We may *fear* that our caring for someone's pain, suffering, or unmet need will be insufficient or incompetent, unhelpful or rejected, upsetting or overwhelming. We may also fear being ridiculed, criticized, or judged. For instance, we may fear our care-giving will be judged as inappropriate, manipulative, or driven by self-interest. Such fears can build up and produce stress as well as fatigue in our caring for others, from others, and for ourselves. Perhaps we are providing homecare to an aunt who has early onset dementia. We soon learn that our aunt's estranged daughter is upset with us and we fear she'll think we took advantage of her mother by pressuring her to come live with us. It is even more upsetting when the daughter criticizes our motives and accuses us of trying to get her mom to change her will. While both the daughter's suspicion and accusation are baseless, we begin to wonder how much longer we can care for our aunt if family tensions escalate.

Blocks to compassion often originate in lack of awareness or knowledge about someone's suffering or how we might respond, along with the contextual factors listed above. For example, increasing caregiving demands may become too exhausting for us to handle or exceed our caring abilities. Moreover, escalating family stress may eventually block our capacity to care for our aunt if she is moved into an out of town assisted living facility.

Examples of *resistances* to feeling and showing compassion include lack of desire to care about someone's misery and withholding of resources due to competition, self-interest, threats, greed, power, or privilege. It is apparent, for instance, that the daughter is creating resistance to our caregiving to her mother through threats, greed, and family pressure. Other examples of resistance include vengeance resulting from strife or arguments and disorders such as depression and schizophrenia. The way such blockages and resistances inhibit compassion is especially well illustrated by clinical psychologist Paul Gilbert and anthropologist Jennifer Mascaro: "We have such limited resources dedicated to the desire for 'every child to grow up in a compassionate environment.' This failure to grasp the size and nature of the problem of 'how children around the world are raised in appalling conditions' is probably humanity's greatest compassion failure."[27]

27. Gilbert and Mascaro, "Compassion Fears, Blocks and Resistances," 405.

As Gilbert and Mascaro point out, recognizing how our evolutionary-driven clash between self-interest and concern for others' well-being is one lens through which to identify and nullify our fears, blocks, and resistances to compassion.[28] Notice how our compassion and concern for our aunt's well-being must be balanced by our own caregiving limitations, her daughter's self-interest, and the escalating family tension. Compassion training has also been found to address these hindrances to compassion, as we'll see in the following section. Moreover, experiencing trust, practicing forgiveness, using power, and managing conflict are each related to dealing with the conflicts of interest that underlie many of our fears, blocks, and resistances to compassion.[29]

It is also helpful to identify compassion risk and protection factors that affect our management of compassion stress and fatigue. Let's consider these causes and antidotes.

Risk and Protection Factors

Trauma scholars, researchers, and practitioners Chares R. Figley and Kathleen Regan Figley identify four risk factors for developing compassion stress and fatigue, and four protection factors to boost compassion stress and fatigue resilience.[30] Risk factors that elevate compassion stress and lower compassion fatigue resilience include:

- Prolonged exposure to suffering
- Traumatic memories
- Empathic stress (from overexposure to suffering, and overextended empathic ability and concern)
- Stressful life events

Protection and resilience factors that offset the impact of compassion stress and fatigue include:

---

28. Gilbert and Mascaro, "Compassion Fears, Blocks and Resistances," 399–418.

29. I address these related topics in *Communication in the Church*. See especially chapters 1, 3, 4, and 5.

30. Figley and Figley, "Compassion Fatigue Resilience," 387–97. It should be noted that these social scientists focus their research on human service workers, including psychologists, social workers, nurses, and physicians. However, their findings may be adapted for use by other helping professionals as well as by all who struggle with compassion stress and fatigue.

- Self-care
- Detachment
- Sense of satisfaction
- Social support

The key to managing compassion stress and fatigue is to be intentional about establishing and maintaining the proper balance between the risk and protection factors. For instance, we can learn to keep our exposure to suffering in check, and to so manage our empathic ability and concern that our compassion response helps others without depleting our capacity to feel and show compassion. We might ask other family members to share in our aunt's care if we're getting exhausted, for example, or ask their help in problem-solving the mounting family tension.

Likewise, feeling our compassionate acts are appreciated can lower a buildup of stress or fatigue arising from our care for someone's suffering. We experience satisfaction and pleasure when our compassion response and helping efforts bring hope to others or a sense of accomplishment to ourselves. Then too, detachment lets us take a physical or mental break from prolonged exposure to suffering or buffer difficult and troubling memories. It can also enable us to disengage from trauma exposure and bounce back from emotional numbness and depression. Think, for instance, of the TV series MASH where Hawkeye and others did crazy things to cope with the stress and constant need to show compassion to injured and dying soldiers.

The ability to detach or set boundaries is often included in self-care plans along with other ways to balance stress and self-care such as:

- A proper diet
- Enough sleep and exercise
- Joy for life
- Meaningful and fulfilling work
- Opportunity for personal growth and professional development

Compassion training, the subject of the section to follow, is one such professional development resource.

A final protective factor to lower unchecked compassion fatigue and boost compassion fatigue resilience is to acquire enough social support such as:

- Peer affirmation
- Mentoring
- Companionship
- Encouragement
- Advice

Compassion Numbness

Related to caregiver burnout and compassion fatigue is numbness to compassion. It is what scholars refer to as "compassion collapse"—the tendency to feel and act more compassionately for a single person than for many people. This tendency toward compassion numbness is particularly evident in public responses to natural disasters, epidemics, genocide, and climate change. Perhaps feeling and showing compassion as individuals on a global scale is an unrealistic expectation. Perhaps there are limits to our compassion and we simply cannot feel compassion for large numbers of victims. Let relief organizations handle large scale disasters, we might conclude. There are, after all, greater financial, material, and emotional costs of showing compassion to many victims than for one victim. For example, there are emotional costs such as becoming exhausted and overwhelmed by the suffering of large numbers.

However, perhaps the benefits of compassionate acts such as the joy we receive from helping a single sufferer are amplified and multiplied by helping larger numbers of sufferers. Moreover, it may be easier to be compassionate in the long term because we are less emotionally involved with many victims compared to the intensive engagement we experience with individual sufferers.

In any event, as social psychologist C. Daryl Cameron suggests, "the scope of compassion is, at least to some extent, under our individual control, depending on what we want to feel. We can choose to expand or contract our bounds of compassion, once we appraise what the costs and benefits of compassion are in each context. If compassion is a choice, then we can motivate change."[31]

---

31. Cameron, "Compassion Collapse," 269.

6. Enhance Compassion.

What motivates us to have a sensitivity or felt response to another's pain or suffering, and a deep or authentic desire to help ease their pain or suffering? Research finds that "the act of helping others—even at a cost to oneself—exists as a natural and even automatic tendency in both animals and humans."[32] In other words, altruism or empathic concern overrides self-interest as a motivation to feel and show compassion. But what factors and processes enhance our tendencies toward compassion, and what type of training enhances our proclivities toward compassion?

Factors and processes that transform relationships of revenge to ones of compassion are illuminating. Research on transforming gang violence, for instance, finds three factors that *push* youth from gangs: being personally hurt, threat of incarceration, and burnout from stress. Three factors that *pull* them out of gangs include: family responsibilities, religious awakening, and parenthood. Likewise, partners in transformational Middle East peace efforts are motivated by such internal personality traits as internal control, optimism, and goal-direction. They may also be motivated by such situational experiences as personally encountered trauma, observance of abuse and degradation, and personal contact with the other side. Finally, transformational peace processes include:

- Humanizing of the other
- Reformulating one's self identity
- Awakening emotionally
- Reconnecting to one's roots
- Dealing with guilt and making amends
- Discovering spirituality anew[33]

Teacher of Buddhist meditation practice Susan Salzberg adds perspective when she states, "We can learn the art of fierce compassion—redefining strength, deconstructing isolation and renewing a sense of community, practicing letting go of rigid us-vs.-them thinking—while cultivating power and clarity in response to difficult situations." Television personality

---

32. Zimbardo et al., "Heroism," 489. Also citing research that shows compassion is deeply rooted in our evolution, brains, biology, and communication is Keltner, "The Compassionate Instinct," 8–15.

33. Zimbardo et al., "Heroism," 490–91.

Ellen DeGeneres adds, "I learned compassion from being discriminated against. Everything bad that's ever happened to me has taught me compassion." And philosopher Eric Hoffer suggests "Compassion is the antitoxin of the soul; where there is compassion even the most poisonous impulses remain relatively harmless."

Next, then, let's look at training efforts that can build our capacity for compassion.

Compassion Training

Developmental psychologists find that parents can teach compassion skills to their children by example, including their style of parenting.[34] As American TV personality Fred Rogers suggests, "Parents are like shuttles on a loom. They join the threads of the past with threads of the future and leave their own bright patterns as they go." Louis Cozolino points out, "The warmth, acceptance, and unconditional positive regard demonstrated in Carl Rogers' work embodies the broad interpersonal environment for the initial growth of the brain and continued development later in life."[35] Commenting further about the neuroscience of parenting, Cozolino says this:

> Primary goals of parenting include providing a child with the capacity for self-soothing and the ability to form positive relationships. This allows the child to face the challenges of life and benefit from healing life experiences. The successful mastery of challenges throughout life leads to taking on even more complex challenges that will promote increasingly high levels of neural network development and integration. When internal or external factors prevent an individual from approaching challenging or stressful situations, the neural systems will tend to remain underdeveloped or unintegrated.[36]

The ability to adapt to changing life circumstances, what neuroscientists call *plasticity*, also is essential. As Cozolino points out, "Plasticity refers to the ability of neurons to change the way they relate to one another as we adapt to the changing demands of life."[37] Indeed, as American cognitive scientist Marvin Minsky reminds us, "The principle activities of brains are

---

34. Keltner, "The Compassionate Instinct," 14–15.
35. Cozolino, *The Neuroscience of Psychotherapy*, 32.
36. Cozolino, *The Neuroscience of Psychotherapy*, 32.
37. Cozolino, *The Neuroscience of Psychotherapy*, 381.

making changes in themselves." And how do people change? Ultimately, concludes Cozolino. "We change by connecting with others while cultivating a deeper relationship with ourselves."[38]

We also learn to cultivate compassion when we see unexpected acts of human goodness, kindness, courage, and compassion, even among strangers, and across cultures and historical eras.[39] Likewise, work environments can motivate compassionate responses.[40] For instance, imagine that your congregation's janitor is exposed to the coronavirus at work and must be quarantined for two weeks. When personnel committee members learn that the janitor only has one week of unused sick leave, their compassionate instincts kick in and they recommend that the board approve an additional week of paid sick leave. At the staff meeting the next day everyone's spirits are lifted when they learn that the board unanimously approved the committee's recommendation. And in appreciation for such an unexpected act of kindness to a colleague, several exuberant staff members feel moved to bring dinner to the janitor's family several times during the next week.

Other social science approaches to enhance compassion focus on two types of training practices: meditation, and responsiveness to change. Research finds that both techniques increase compassionate thoughts, feelings, intentions, motivations, and responses to suffering and pain. Mindfulness- and compassion-based meditation practices that increase compassionate outcomes include training sessions with certified instructors, often from Buddhist traditions.[41] Expert guidance using web- and mobile-based

---

38. Cozolino, *The Neuroscience of Psychotherapy*, 433.

39. Haidt, "Wired to Be Inspired," 86–93. Also see Swain and Ho, "Parental Brain," 65–77; and Kirby, "Compassion-Focused Parenting," 91–105.

40. Suttie, "Compassion Across Cubicles," 133–39.

41. For example, the Dalai Lama, in a conversation on global compassion with psychologist Paul Ekman, says the Buddhist meditation practice of compassion begins with reflecting deeply upon the downside of narrow-minded self-centeredness. Then one reflects on the positive consequences and potential of more other-centered perspectives. Through these reflections, one cultivates compassion. For more information about this conversation, see Ekman, "Global Compassion: A Conversation Between the Dalai Lama and Paul Ekman," 278. And then in *An Open Heart*, 91–106, the Dalai Lama suggests that we cultivate the transformative attitude and practice of compassion by opening our heart through empathy and closeness to others, and by training our mind through a profound understanding and recognition of our own and others' suffering. Moreover, in *How to Be Compassionate,* 8 and 84, the Dalai Lama reminds us that the ultimate purpose of a transformative warmhearted and mental practice of compassion is to help ourselves and all humanity overcome suffering and find happiness. Similarly, in a daily meditation on contemplation, "The Source of Action," Jesuit priest Richard Rohr points out that Jesus

technologies also facilitate engagement in contemplative practices. Fortunately, meditation-based training is effective in strengthening both compassion for oneself and compassion for others.[42]

Non-meditation-based techniques that also prove effective for boosting compassion include responsiveness to change. As English naturalist, biologist, and geologist Charles Darwin reminds us, "It is not the strongest of the species that survive, not the most intelligent, but the one most responsive to change." Or, as Japanese martial artist Morihei Ueshiba remarks, "Life is growth. If we stop growing technically and spiritually, we're as good as dead." Responsiveness to change that increases compassion includes identification with a stranger's plight and awareness of helping behaviors to alleviate the suffering. A sense of similarity with other individuals is also a viable way to extend compassion beyond one's in-group and to reduce bias for helping one's in-group. Moreover, felt security that bolsters compassionate response to someone's suffering includes recalling help in times of need from a parent, close friend, or partner. Further research is needed to determine if meditation practice and responsiveness to change help in overcoming compassion fatigue.[43]

One other approach to cultivate compassion is a compassion-based skills training program. Intended outcomes of this educational intervention program are an increase in compassion for others and a reduction in fears of compassion from others, for others, and for self. Such fears include feeling undeserving compassion or feeling that compassion is a weakness. This approach aims to enhance one's understanding of compassion as well as one's sense of resilience, empathy, and compassion toward oneself

---

and other great spiritual teachers also emphasize the transformation of consciousness and soul, of mind and heart, as a basis for social action rooted in compassion, humility, and patience. Finally, Gilbert presents compassionate mind training featuring exercises to develop compassion attributes and skills to counteract the feelings, thinking, and behaviors of our threat and self-protection system in *The Compassionate Mind*, chapters 6–13.

42. Neff and Germer, "Self-Compassion and Psychological Well-being," 379–80.

43. For more information about these two types of training practices for building our capacity for compassion, including findings from research, see Condon and DeSteno, "Enhancing Compassion," 287–98. For additional related information in *The Oxford Handbook of Compassion Science*, see Lavelle, "Compassion in Context," 17–25; Weng et al., "The Impact of Compassion Meditation Training," 133–46; Skwara et al., "Studies of Training Compassion," 219–36; Goldin and Jazaieri, "Compassion Cultivation Training," 237–45; Mascaro et al., "Cognitively Based Compassion Training," 247–57; Mikulincer and Shaver, "Adult Attachment and Compassion," 79–89; and Lavelle et al., "A Call for Compassion and Care," 475–85.

and others. Participants are exposed to cutting-edge, evidence-based literature on well-being and compassion, and then engage in peer-to-peer discussion on pertinent topics. Results of a pilot study in hospitals and universities reported by Daniel Martin and Yotam Heineberg are promising, and research is on-going.[44]

7. Cultivating Compassion is Connected to Social Justice.

Buddhist scholar and Tibetan political leader Lobsang Tenzin comments, "A compassionate mind is very difficult to cultivate because compassion demands a sense of equality between all living beings." His assertion is backed by research. Indeed, social science research on cultivating compassion finds an important connection to social justice. For example, the unequal sharing and unsustainable use of world resources by powerful nations is an obstacle to developing global compassion.[45] Research also is showing "that cultivating compassion could have more widespread effects on all kinds of social behaviors, including behavior crucial for norm reinforcement and justice in societies."[46] Indeed, "Compassion is a powerful feature of human experience and is a key component of individual, interpersonal, organizational, and societal well-being."[47] However, while the connection between compassion and social justice is acknowledged by social scientists, more studies are needed to understand how compassion training influences the interactions between privileged and under-represented groups, high and low political power in groups, and wealthy and poor levels of society.[48]

Paul Gilbert's compassionate-mind training recognizes the importance of compassion in counteracting the inhumane tendencies of

---

44. Martin and Heineberg, "Social Dominance and Leadership," 495–506.

45. This point is highlighted in the dialogue between the Dalai Lama and Paul Ekman cited in footnote 41, and by the Dalai Lama in *An Open Heart*, 14–15. Also see Piff and Moskowitz, "The Class-Compassion Gap: How Socioeconomic Factors Influence Compassion," 317–30.

46. Klimecki and Singer, "The Compassionate Brain," 118.

47. Goldin and Jazaieri, "Compassionate Cultivation Training," 237. Also making this point in *The Oxford Handbook of Compassion Science* are Weng et al., "The Impact of Compassion Meditation Training on the Brain and Prosocial Behavior," 133; Carter et al, "The Roots of Compassion," 173; and Koopman-Holm and Tsai, "The Cultural Shaping of Compassion," 273.

48. Goldin and Jazaierik 'Compassionate Cultivation Training," 244.

retributive justice with the healing power of restorative justice.[49] And Scottish Roman Catholic Cardinal Keith O'Brien advocates a system of justice based on a culture of compassion rather than on a culture of vengeance. Likewise, professor of theology and social ethics Maureen O'Connell affirms that the purpose of compassion "is restorative justice for the entire community, or a renewal of the community's capability to flourish through a renewed capacity for relationality."[50] She goes on to comment: "Compassion overrides social, cultural, racial, economic, and religious boundaries. It accepts personal accountability for the stranger-turned-neighbor and stops at nothing to ensure that person's physical and emotional well-being. It brings disparate people together in a personal, embodied, and emotional relationship."[51] O'Connell calls for a holistic and transformative response to unjust suffering with these characteristics:

- Honest assessment of what is required for suffering people to flourish
- Awareness of direct or indirect collusion in the causes of suffering
- Understanding the reality of those who suffer
- Active commitment to human flourishing rooted in resisting causes of suffering and in finding solutions for alleviating suffering[52]

Commenting further about the transformative power of relationships for human flourishing,[53] O'Connell says, "It is precisely in the context of relationship that compassion promises transformative possibilities for both the suffering and non-suffering persons:

- Compassion recognizes our inherent vulnerability, particularly vulnerabilities that lie outside the control of some but squarely under the control of others.
- Compassionate responses aim to empower us to overcome unjustly imposed vulnerabilities through increased capacity for relationship with self and others.

---

49. Gilbert, *The Compassionate Mind*, 240–44. More will be said about these two types of justice (retributive and restorative) in chapter 6, Doing Justice.

50. O'Connell, *Compassion: Loving Our Neighbor*, 67.

51. O'Connell, *Compassion: Loving Our Neighbor*, 70.

52. O'Connell, *Compassion: Loving Our Neighbor*, 91.

53. It is important to keep in mind that compassion includes focus on individuals *and* systems, causes *and* consequences, reflections *and* actions, nature *and* nurture, and contexts local *and* global.

- Compassion can be the virtue that stimulates, evaluates, and directs transformative relationality, particularly on a global scale."[54]

American author Susan Vreeland links our relationships, compassion, and justice with this concluding thought: "Where there is no human connection, there is no compassion. Without compassion, then community, commitment, loving-kindness, human understanding, and peace all shrivel. Individuals become isolated, the isolated turn cruel, and the tragic hovers in the forms of domestic and civil violence."[55] Or, in the words of civil rights leader Coretta Scott King, "We can prevent many people from becoming terrorists by truly listening to people who feel they've been treated unjustly and responding to their concerns with a sense of justice and compassion."

Summary and Conclusion

Compassion is the feeling aroused by an awareness of someone's challenging circumstances that threaten their well-being. Often, though not always, our heart-felt concern for someone's pain, unjust suffering, or unmet need results in a desire to show our care in ways that help them thrive or flourish anew. Sometimes, though, we may be more upset by someone's suffering than for their suffering. Self-inflicted suffering may lessen our motivation to show compassion as might challenging circumstances that overwhelm us even with our intervention. Our own exposure to dangerous or threatening situations or our feelings of inadequacy to help may also cause us to reappraise, block, regulate, or limit our care giving motivation and behavior.

Next, we learned that our brains are wired to thrive on compassion. They have evolved to be caring and to need caring. In fact, our brains shape our caring response to suffering even as our relationships with others shape our brain's response to suffering.

Just as we feel and show compassion to others, so also do we need to feel and practice compassion for ourselves when we are the suffering person. We need to remember that everyone suffers, be kind to ourselves, and be mindful to take the position of concern for the other towards ourselves. Numerous benefits are associated with treating ourselves with inner kindness rather than with inner neglect.

---

54. O'Connell, *Compassion: Loving Our Neighbor*, 98.
55. From brainyquote.com.

Organizations as well as individuals can respond to pain and suffering with compassion.

Because our experience of compassion can result in high levels of stress and fatigue, we considered role-related conditions and contextual factors. We also examined fears, blocks, and resistances that can inhibit compassion. Next, we identified risk, protection, and reduction factors that affect our management of compassion stress and fatigue. And we examined ways to handle compassion numbness. Compassion is a choice we make by balancing the demands compassion makes on us with the abilities and resources we need to help alleviate someone's suffering.

Since compassion is a skill to be learned, we examined the factors and the processes that enhance our tendencies toward compassion, along with types of training that can cultivate our capacities for compassion.

Finally, since compassion is connected to social justice, we explored the transformative power of relationships to overcome unjust suffering and to promote human flourishing, both individually and globally.

The seven guidelines of practical wisdom and best practices presented in this chapter reveal how feeling compassion offers us better ways for our relationships to flourish during times of crises, as well as in life's everyday challenges. Indeed, feeling and showing compassion has the power to transform human hurt into human well-being and thriving.

Practical Applications

1. Recall an experience of someone's pain or suffering. How did you respond in terms of your feelings, thoughts, and behaviors? What factors affected your motivation, desire, and willingness to show compassion? How does your congregation respond to people's pain or suffering? What factors would affect its showing of compassion?

2. How does your brain affect your responses to someone's pain or suffering? What impact do your caring relationships have on your brain's response to someone's suffering?

3. How have you experienced compassion when the one suffering is yourself? How kind were you, or could you have been, to yourself? How can the practice of mindfulness be useful? How does your congregation respond when it is suffering?

4. What do you see as the benefits of compassion, including self-compassion?

5. Think of instances where compassion was, or could have been, part of an organization's culture? What can you do to promote a culture of compassion in an organization of which you are a part?

6. How have you or your congregation experienced and managed compassion stress, fatigue, and numbness? Notice which compassion inhibitors, risk and prevention factors, and coping mechanisms were or were not present.

7. What are several ways you and members of your congregation can enhance your compassion skills?

8. What connection do you see between cultivating compassion and doing social justice?

For Further Study

Cozolino, Louis. *The Neuroscience of Human Relationships: Attachment and the Developing Social Brain*, 3rd ed. (New York: Norton, 2017).

The Dalai Lama. *An Open Heart: Practicing Compassion in Everyday Life*, Nicholas Vreeland, ed. (New York: Back Bay, 2001).

———. *How to Be Compassionate: A Handbook for Creating Inner Peace and a Happier World*, Jeffrey Hopkins, trans., and ed. (New York: Atria, 2011).

Gilbert, Paul. *The Compassionate Mind: A New Approach to Life's Challenges* (London: Robinson, 2013).

Keltner, Dacher, Jason Marsh, and Jeremy Adam Smith, eds. *The Compassionate Instinct: The Science of Human Goodness* (New York: Norton, 2010).

Seppala, Emma M., Emiliana Simon-Thomas, Stephanie L. Brown, Monica C. Worline, C. Daryl Cameron, and James R. Doty, eds. *The Oxford Handbook of Compassion Science* (New York: Oxford University Press, 2017).

Chapter 4

Showing Kindness

Love is kind.—1 Corinthians 13:4

If there were a single practice capable of transforming person and planet, it would be kindness.—Rami Shapiro

A clergy couple's family is saving money to qualify for a new home loan. They would like to build a cedar home for which they would have to act as their own general contractor. Since they are a little shy on their loan down payment, a bank agrees to let the couple acquire their own subcontractors with the guidance of an experienced builder. Midway through the building process, the stress of working with subcontractors on top of his regular full-time pastoral responsibilities results in the husband having a mental breakdown, leaving the contracting work to his spouse. With two preschool children for which to care, full-time responsibilities of her own, a husband hospitalized with clinical depression to visit, and on-going house contracting responsibilities, the spouse finds herself in full crisis mode. When people from their congregation become aware of their pastors' trauma, members of a Bible study group offer to bring meals several times a week. Retirees unexpectedly volunteer to watch the couple's children after school. Building committee members step forward to help with finishing work and removal of surplus material. Relationships deepen through multiple unexpected little acts of kindness by several dozen members of the congregation, without which the couple's home would never have been completed on time as required by their bank. Lives and relationships are transformed. They are doing what English writer and philosopher Aldous Huxley recommends: "Try to be a little kinder." Or, in relational terms, a way of life American novelist Henry James enthusiastically endorses:

"Three things in human life are important. The first is to be kind. The second is to be kind. And the third is to be kind."

But what leads us to live into our better selves? What is it about kindness that transforms relationships? In this chapter, you'll find four guidelines of practical wisdom to learn how kindness offers us better ways for our relationships to flourish in everyday life challenges as well in times of vulnerability and crisis. Also, look for best practices gleaned from recent research for how acts of kindness give you the power to transform your relationships for the better in your congregation.

Guidelines for Showing Kindness

1. Love Kindly.

As a Buddhist, the Dalai Lama says, "My religion is very simple. My religion is kindness." He also comments, "Be kind whenever possible. It is always possible." Lovingkindness is the Buddhist practice of *metta*—a way of gently befriending. In chapter 1 we saw that loving kindness, or perhaps more accurately, loving kindly, is inextricably linked to doing justice and walking humbly in the Judeo-Christian tradition. Each depends on and reinforces the other. Perhaps the best way to love kindly is to deeply desire and tenacious commit ourselves to one another's well-being. In his book, *What Does the Lord Require? Doing Justice, Loving Kindness, Walking Humbly*, James C. Howell describes loving kindness as "the way a newlywed looks at the wedding ring and the promises made: being bound is freedom finally found; there is nothing I wouldn't promise or do for you."[1] Psychologist and theologian Sharon Parks speaks of being loved tenderly, fiercely, and tenaciously in response to our human vulnerabilities. She suggests loving "with an awareness of the capacity of the other to be wounded, to suffer pain, and to be dependent upon relationship with others. To love tenderly requires a particular capacity of spirit and an informed sensitivity."[2] To cope with life's vulnerabilities Parks believes we need nurturing environments that *hold* us, networks of belonging that *ground* us, and communities of contradiction that *challenge* us.

The Apostle Paul says succinctly and simply, "Love is kind." Clinical psychologist Tara Cousineau similarly defines kindness as love in action.

---

1. Howell, *What Does the Lord Require?*, 48.
2. Parks, "Love Tenderly," 30.

"It is any act of love that reflects genuine caring. Such kindheartedness is the embodiment of your feelings of warmth and generosity toward others and the world at large—and your desire to bring relief to those who are suffering. In this way, kindness is both a quality of loving presence and an orientation to life that is intentional and active."[3] And it is more important now than ever before, because it breaks down barriers that separate us such as class, religion, ethnicity, gender, and disability. Kindness affirms people and sees the goodness in them. As Rabbi Rami Shapiro puts it, "If there were a single practice capable of transforming person and planet, it would be kindness."

In the early days of the novel coronavirus pandemic facemasks were not readily available, even though their use was recommended in public places. It was weeks into the pandemic, for example, that I was able to obtain one. In an act of incalculable kindness, the aunt of our local produce market owner began making facemasks and donating them to her nephew's business. Customers were invited to take one for free even though they each cost around $2.00 to make. In lieu of payment customers were invited to make a cash donation to our local food bank. Along with many other customers, I was eager to show my appreciation for finally obtaining a facemask by making a generous donation to help needy neighbors find food. Kindness was contagious! Even as the coronavirus is contagious, so also is showing kindness. An aunt's act of loving kindness for her community prompted a produce owner to show kindness to his customers, kindness that customers eagerly passed on to neighbors in need.

Social science research finds that our acts of random kindness are intentional behaviors or practices that increase, enhance, and sustain happiness in others.[4] It is what Princess Diana is getting at when she said, "Carry out a random act of kindness, with no expectation of reward, safe in the knowledge that one day someone might do the same for you." Other life-transforming benefits of showing kindness identified by social scientists, some of which may surprise you, include:

- Activating emotional regulation and compassion networks in the brain
- Alleviating symptoms related to depression and post-traumatic stress disorder in veterans

---

3. Cousineau, *The Kindness Cure*, 11.
4. Boehm and Lyubomirsky, "The Promise of Sustainable Happiness," 671–72.

- Protecting against compassion fatigue in helping professionals and first responders
- Lessening migraines and symptoms of chronic pain
- Promoting positive attitudes and compassion toward oneself and others
- Lessening judgment and increasing empathy for stigmatized social groups
- Improving body image
- Strengthening romantic relationships
- Improving symptoms related to depression, anxiety, and social isolation in teenagers
- Fostering stress resilience and prosocial behaviors in young children
- Promoting longevity in those who volunteer[5]

2. Kindness is Powerful.

"When facing anything that feels threatening—be it political, personal, or as natural as a life change—you can 'kill' your fears with kindness."[6] So says Tara Cousineau about the power of kindness to transform our relationships marred by fear and threat to ones of thriving and well-being. All too often in modern society, though, she observes that kindness is associated with being weak, fragile, nostalgic, and untrustworthy. Fortunately, even as we learned in chapter 3 about our brains being wired to thrive on compassion, so too, says Cousineau, "our instinct for kindness percolates to the surface all the time, because our basic neurology is wired to care."[7] However, she reminds us that it takes effort to transform kindness from a sentimental mindset to a natural expression of love, respect, and appreciation: "you possess a compassionate instinct. It's part of your genetic blueprint. But the capacity for kindness can erode if you don't exercise it."[8]

So how *do* we exercise this quality? Let's turn, then, to practical guidance for learning better ways to cultivate our kindness instinct. Expect these

---

5. Reported by Cousineau in *The Kindness Cure*, 6.
6. Cousineau, *The Kindness Cure*, 4.
7. Cousineau, *The Kindness Cure*, 4.
8. Cousineau, *The Kindness Cure*, 4.

loving-kindness practices and skills to help transform your relationships with yourself and others into a life filled with meaning, satisfaction, and well-being. The perspective of clinical psychologist Louis Cozolino about change, in chapter 3, is worth repeating here: "We change by connecting with others while cultivating a deeper relationship with ourselves."[9]

3. Cultivate Kindness.

In chapter 3 we examined training efforts to build our capacity for compassion. Some of the same parenting recommendations, mindfulness mediation practices, and skill-building training programs may be adapted for use in cultivating kindness.[10]

Mindful of popular TV talk show host Ellen DeGeneres' trademark farewell, "Be kind to one another," recall acts of kindness you have shown to others and to yourself. How about kindness you've received from yourself and others, or witnessed among people in your congregation? Imagine how these acts can be repeated, expanded, and adopted. As you reflect on these instances, ask yourself, how well do you do in showing kindness? How frequently and effectively do others show kindness to you? How about people in general, and people in your congregation in particular?

Perhaps the most obvious and effective way to cultivate kindness is to engage our powers of observation and our instincts for caring. For example, our awareness, curiosity, presence, listening, empathy, and generosity communicate and express our care. They offer comfort and create a sense of community and connection. While these expressions of kindness are useful in our congregations and everyday lives, they take on greater importance in times of threat, trauma, and stress. We see such acts performed repeatedly by members of the pastors' congregation throughout their homebuilding crisis. In sum, showing kindness helps sustain life, connect and reconnect with others, raise self-esteem, inspire confidence, offer security and support, solve problems, and make decisions that promote well-being and human flourishing—both in ourselves and for others.

Often acts of kindness go beyond what our culture would normally expect or require of us. Let's say we stopped in the rain to help a young

---

9. Cozolino, *The Neuroscience of Psychotherapy*, 433.

10. You may also want to do the same with such skills as building relationships, experiencing trust, practicing forgiveness, and using power—topics I cover in *Communication in the Church*, chapters 1, 3, 4, and 5.

mom with two toddlers in the car that's got a flat tire. People wouldn't think we were evil if we drove on by. But it's kindness that pushes us to go beyond what is expected of us.

So, sensitivity, curiosity, and tenderness cultivate our instinctual and natural capacities for kindness. They engage the neuro plasticity of our minds—*the ability of our minds to shape our experience and the ability of our experience to shape our minds*. Tara Cousineau's experience as a clinical psychologist, teacher of meditation, and kindness researcher leads her to say: "[W]e can lay down neural networks for kindness. We can engage systematic practices that cultivate feelings of compassion and communities of caring."[11] Thereby our acts of kindness transform our relationships with ourselves and others from human need to human flourishing. Let's consider, then, particularly useful ways to cultivate kindness.

Curiosity

To show kindness, we need to become aware of opportunities. We must become acquainted with and sensitive to the life situations of ourselves and others, both in the moment and beyond. And how do we become so aware of these life experiences that we discover opportunities for showing kindness?

One way is through our curiosity. It is a way of being interested in one another's interests, a way of being aware and becoming acquainted. It is a way of paying attention to others' life circumstances and being aware of opportunities for expressing acts of kindness when appropriate.

For instance, imagine that you have just fastened your seatbelt for an airplane flight and are seated next to a stranger. Typically, we turn to our seatmate with a smile, say "hello," and engage in polite chitchat as we await take off. Our curiosity in one another's interests may lead us to further conversation after our initial introductions and exchange of pleasantries. We may be curious about where we are each going, the purpose of our travels, our hometowns and occupations. We may learn that our seatmate is on an important business trip or on the way to visit a longtime friend. Upon arrival at our destination and as we depart, we may say to our new acquaintance, "I hope your meeting goes well," or "It was good to meet you. I hope you have a great time with your friend." In other words,

---

11. Cousineau, *The Kindness Cure*, 10.

we wish them well. In reply, we're told, "Gee, thanks. I appreciate your kind words. The best to you, too!"

Notice that the relationship between seatmates is transformed from stranger to acquaintance through a simple smile and curiosity in one another's interests. And through becoming aware of basic information about one another's lives we take our leave of one another with expressions of appreciation for having met and of wishing one another well.

Thoughtfulness

Now, imagine that the reason for your plane trip is to attend the memorial service of a parent or close friend. We may or may not have shared this personal information with our seatmate. It probably depends on how curious our seatmate was about us, what is important in our life, and where we were in our grief process at the time.

Upon arrival you are met by your sister and learn that the director of your mom's assisted living facility just today returned from vacation and learned of your mom's passing. Your sister shows you this email from the director: "I was sad to hear about your mom's passing! I just returned from vacation and learned that your mom died while I was away. I've known your mom for many years and knew your dad, too, before he died. They were a lovely couple. Your mom was a spunky, fun-loving person with a big heart. I will miss seeing her and I will miss seeing you and your sister, too. Blessings."

In response to this heartfelt expression of care and comfort, your sister shows you her reply: "Thank you for your kind thoughts and words about both mom and dad. If I remember correctly, you were the first person to meet and welcome them when they moved from their home to assisted living. You were always so kind to them and our family is deeply grateful for your thoughtfulness. Take special care and God bless!"

It should be noted here that both what we say to people and how we say it matters. What we say should be helpful rather than hurtful. It should be truthful and not misleading, necessary without causing harm, and beneficial but not overwhelming. And how we speak should include being thoughtful, careful, kindly, and motivated by our good intentions and other people's best interests.

Sometimes we feel as though we don't know what to do when someone needs help. While every situation is unique and requires discernment to determine how best to help someone in need, there are some general guidelines to follow. Here are some do's and don'ts:

Do's

- Be supportive
- Be caring
- Be thoughtful
- Be present
- Listen
- Offer specific help
- Be creative
- Empower

Don'ts

- Be judgmental
- Give advice unless asked
- Expect to be asked for help
- Try to solve or fix someone's problem
- Use lack of money as an excuse
- Presume you know how someone feels
- Tell someone what they should or shouldn't feel
- Tell someone to get over it
- Tell someone to learn from the experience or something good will come from it[12]

Generosity

The song title, *Kind and Generous*, assumes and expresses an important connection between kindness and generosity. How, though, are these behaviors related? Generosity is simply acting kindly, with abundance. Generosity is

---

12. Adapted from Johnson, *The Kindness Handbook*, 1–5.

kindness writ large. Often generosity originates with thankfulness and expresses itself in grateful, thoughtful acts of kindness.

Like compassion, generosity and kindness also can be contagious. They activate our mirror neurons, our natural capacity to copy another person's behavior. Mental health counselor and social work professor Wendy Lustbader says, "When it is most fruitful, kindness is passed on in the form of generosity toward others. Jaded people who have lived only for themselves begin to take an interest in those around them, having discovered the worth of mercy through their own vulnerability. Bitter people begin to experiment with nurturance, having tasted something of its satisfactions when they were ill."[13]

In her clinical practice, Lustbader observes that generosity is sustainable and a key to a good life well lived: "People with a history of generous exchanges with others tend to carry these inclinations with them to the end of their lives. Wherever they live, whatever they do, they readily make connections with other people and derive satisfaction from doing so. When frailty encroaches, they tend to be surrounded by loyal helpers. There can be no certain formula for security, but kindness is rarely wasted and the habit of generosity almost always serves as a strength."[14] The coronavirus pandemic facemask scenario cited earlier demonstrates many of these same dynamics.

Normally, generosity is thought to be a good thing with no down side. It is usually greatly appreciated and highly valued. Indeed, non-profit organizations cannot operate and flourish without the generosity of their volunteers' time, talent, and money. Moreover, generosity need not be reciprocated to create healthy relationships; rather, it is freely given without expectation of reward or obligation. Then too, a lifestyle of kindness and generosity is a source of hope, as Lustbader notes: "The expectation that we will be able to count on kindness during our time of need becomes one of life's most sustaining convictions. We hope that if we become incapacitated, our friends and relatives will stand by us. We hope that their help will arise out of affection rather than out of pity, and that we will bear our difficulties gracefully enough to keep on inspiring their loyalty. We suspect that the measure of a good life is how we are treated at the end."[15]

---

13. Lustbader, *Counting on Kindness*, 174.
14. Lustbader, *Counting on Kindness*, 177.
15. Lustbader, *Counting on Kindness*, 180.

Richard Davidson is a neuroscientist and founder of the Center for Healthy Minds at the University of Wisconsin, Madison. He suggests that the practice of generosity, along with kindness and compassion, promotes well-being in our lives. He says, "There are now a plethora of data showing that when individuals engage in generous and altruistic behavior, they actually activate circuits in the brain that are key to fostering well-being. These circuits get activated in a way that is more enduring than the way we respond to other positive incentives, such as winning a game or earning a prize."[16] He also finds evidence that the practices of lovingkindness and compassion activate brain circuits that promote well-being by taking a positive outlook on life. Davidson describes this outlook as "the ability to see the positive in others, the ability to savor positive experiences, the ability to see another human being as a human being who has innate basic goodness."[17]

Pausing

In an article on faith and leadership, "Practicing kindness in the midst of rage," Duke Divinity School administrator Alaina Kleinbeck imagines Jesus counting to 10 in order to practice kindness amid profound anger. She comments, "When Jesus experienced rage, he did not dehumanize, insult or disparage. Instead of responding with violence, Jesus offered grace, mercy and kindness. Jesus welcomed both oppressed and oppressor, without judgment, to be with him, to eat and learn with him, to experience a different way of being. When Jesus saw people for who they could be and invited them to follow, he was holding his rage and kindness together in powerful and sacred ways."[18] Pausing before reacting with anger, defensiveness, intolerance, impatience, or threats can enable us to take in more of the situation and to become mindful about the reasons for our hostile tendencies. And it can allow us opportunity to practice kindness amid our experience of rage as well.

Consider the situation where someone has the chronic, annoying habit of dominating group discussion. Typically, such monopolizing of communication results in group members becoming frustrated by their inability to contribute to group discussion, solve problems, and make decisions.

---

16. Davidson, "The Four Keys to Well-Being." Along with generosity, Davidson identifies resilience, outlook, and attention as the four keys to well-being.

17. Davidson, "The Four Keys to Well-Being."

18. Kleinbeck, "Practicing Kindness in the Midst of Rage."

Member participation and satisfaction, along with group productivity, often wane. What would happen, though, if you as a group leader or member paused before becoming frustrated, and, instead became curious and mindful about what is leading the dominator to control group interaction and curb group effectiveness? In a moment of reflection, it occurs to you to invite the dysfunctional group member to lunch or out for coffee. Opportunity to get better acquainted leads you to listen to each other's life story. You learn that your conversational partner came from an abusive homelife, has virtually no friends, and cannot keep a job. It occurs to you that this dysfunctional group member is really a fearful, lonely outsider, and constantly worries about even the bare necessities of life. This individual is doing everything possible to lead a normal life. Your natural capacity for understanding, empathy, compassion, and kindness kick in and your relationship is transformed from a desire to distance yourself to a desire to reach out with empathic listening, compassionate concern, and kindheartedness. Initially, it may not curb dominating group behavior, but it can transform your response from cringing and repulsion to patience and creative problem-solving. Moreover, the next time your group meets, you decide to sensitively interrupt the dominator, express curiosity about other members' perspectives, and invite contributions from other members of the group. Your awareness that the dominating individual is likely trying to be a good group member enables your group to set conversational boundaries and adopt member participation practices that can transform group dysfunction into healthy group discussion and decision making.

Indeed, traumatic events in our lives trigger stress, alter immune systems, and affect brain chemistry. Our needs for safety and self-esteem, for belonging and bridging cultures skyrocket. And our acts of kindness toward vulnerable people are vital for their survival and for helping restore their flourishing. A simple phone call, note, or visit. A listening ear, warm smile, or shared meal. A car ride or fun activity. All can have an important, transformative impact. So can nonverbal behaviors such as appropriate touch or engaged facial expressions. Comfortable eye contact and varied tone of voice can also play a role. Then too, our attention and presence communicate our care. Our listening and empathy create a sense of community. Our generosity offers comfort. Such kind-hearted efforts and behaviors help sustain life, connect and reconnect with others, and raise self-esteem. And they provide support, help solve problems, and foster good decision-making.

4. Kindness is Related to Compassion, Joy, and Equanimity.

Earlier in this chapter we learned that lovingkindness may be understood from the Buddhist tradition as gentle befriending. Such boundless openheartedness especially expresses itself through four relational qualities: kindness, compassion, joy, and equanimity (balance, poise, or liberation). Here is how Buddhist scholar and teacher Christina Feldman describes the way these four qualities are related:

> Kindness, compassion, joy, and equanimity are a family of qualities that support, strengthen, nourish, and balance one another. Immeasurable kindness teaches us a way of being in this world that is no longer defined by ideas of friends and enemies, by likes and dislikes, preferences and demands for reciprocation. Boundless friendliness is the root of compassion and protects it from despair and partiality. Kindness guards equanimity from falling into indifference.
>
> Compassion protects kindness from falling into sentimentality or becoming only a state of elation, always recollecting the reality of the immensity of sorrow in the world. Compassion, rooted in kindness, becomes selfless and protects joy from forgetfulness. Compassion extends the remit of kindness and turns it into altruistic and healing action.
>
> Joy is needed to temper the raw edges of sorrow and pain encountered as our hearts tremble in the face of sorrow and anguish. Joy brings ease and rest into our endeavors to bring the origins of suffering to an end. The joyful heart tempers pain and suffering with the remembering of that which is well and unbroken, even in the midst of distress, and guards the compassionate heart from being overwhelmed by sorrow.
>
> Equanimity brings to kindness and compassion patience and steadiness; equanimity balances joy, protecting it from wandering into the emotional extremes of exuberance, just as joy softens and brings serenity to equanimity. Equanimity allows us to act without becoming preoccupied with the results and outcomes of our actions. It is a quality of strength and inner poise that allows us to respond to the world of experience without fear and hesitation.[19]

On the one hand, selfish affection and painful ill will obstruct kindness. Pity and cruelty impede compassion. Exuberance and resentment limit joy. Indifference and clinging inhibit equanimity. On the other hand, positive

---

19. Feldman, *Boundless Heart*, 2–3.

feelings of warmth and tenderness flow from kindness. Deep care, connectedness, and responsiveness from compassion. Gladness, aliveness, and vitality from joy. Poise, balance, and steadiness from equanimity.

Feldman offers this hopeful conclusion: "In this fragile life, so easily broken and riven by affliction, we come to see that it is only kindness, compassion, joy, and equanimity that make sense. As the Buddha put it, 'Whether standing, sitting, walking or lying down we abide in kindness, compassion, joy, and equanimity. There is no more noble way to live in this world.' This is the essence of a liberated heart, rooted in unshakeable kindness, compassion, joy, and equanimity."[20]

Summary and Conclusion

Kindness is love in action. Loving kindly is beneficial and it is powerful. The practice of showing kindness transforms relationships by triggering neurons in our brains that lead us to act compassionately, generously, and thoughtfully. Thereby, depression, fear, isolation, and anxiety are alleviated. Resiliency from stress and fatigue is increased. Positive attitudes towards us and others is promoted. Prosocial behaviors are fostered. Defensive and destructive behaviors are averted. Empathy is cultivated, prejudice and intolerance overcome, and listening activated. Body image is improved. Intimacy and affection are strengthened, well-being fostered, and longevity improved.

Many ways to show kindness are identified. Practical ways to cultivate kindness include curiosity, thoughtfulness, generosity, and pausing to guard against our hostile tendencies.

Behaviors that harm relationships such as anger, defensiveness, judgment, intolerance, impatience, and threats can be transformed into helpful relationship behaviors. Behaviors such as warmth and supportiveness, openness and acceptance, patience and care.

Transformative, boundless, liberating openheartedness is fostered through kindness along with three inter-related relational qualities, including compassion, joy, and equanimity.

The four guidelines of practical wisdom and best practices presented in this chapter reveal how showing kindness offers us better ways for our relationships to flourish in our congregations and everyday lives as well as

20. Feldman, *Boundless Heart*, 144.

during times of need that threaten our well-being. Indeed, showing kindness has the power to transform human need into human thriving.

Practical Applications

1. Identify specific ways you do and do not show kindness to yourself and to others? How about people in general? How about your congregation?
2. What are several positive impacts and benefits that showing kindness has on your relationships and your overall well-being? How about such impacts and benefits of showing kindness on relationships in your congregation and on its overall well-being?
3. What guidelines for helping people in need are most useful for discerning how best to show kindness for you and for your congregation?
4. Review the suggestions for cultivating kindness, and then identify those that strike you as most useful for you and for your congregation.
5. What connections between kindness, compassion, joy, and equanimity are most useful for transforming harmful or dysfunctional behaviors in your relationships into behaviors that bring relational health and well-being? How about in your congregation?

For Further Study

Brueggemann, Walter, Sharon Parks, and Thomas H. Groome. *To Act Justly, Love Tenderly, Walk Humbly: An Agenda for Ministers* (Eugene, OR: Wipf & Stock, 1997).

Cousineau, Tara. *The Kindness Cure: How the Science of Compassion Can Heal Your Heart & Your World* (Oakland, CA: New Harbinger, 2018).

Feldman, Christina. *Boundless Heart: The Buddha's Path of Kindness, Compassion, Joy, and Equanimity* (Boulder, CO: Shambhala, 2017).

Johnson, Jeri-Lynn. *The Kindness Handbook: When You Want to Help But Don't Know What to Do* (Salt Lake City: Shadow Mountain, 2001).

Lustbader, Wendy. *Counting on Kindness: The Dilemmas of Dependency* (New York: Free Press, 1991).

Neafsey, John. *Act Justly, Love Tenderly: Lifelong Lessons in Conscience and Calling* (Maryknoll, NY: Orbis, 2016).

Chapter 5

Expressing Appreciation

The deepest craving of human nature is the need to be appreciated. —William James

Encourage one other and build up each other.
—1 Thessalonians 5:11

As your congregation's education ministry team considers a new curriculum for your children's Sunday school program, a memory from your early childhood education catches you by surprise. You remember getting back a spelling test with five wrong answers circled in red ink. As you think back, it occurs to you that you cannot recall ever taking a similar test and seeing twenty-five correct answers circled in green ink. When such early children learning experiences were repeated in myriad ways over the years, you learned what you do poorly more than what you do well. Consequently, you've gotten a skewed, unbalanced, and inaccurate view of yourself. Unfortunately, as this type of feedback became the norm, you developed a lower view of yourself than is accurate and needlessly suffer from low self-esteem.

When your attention returns to choosing a new Sunday school curriculum, you remember the Apostle Paul expressing his appreciation for the congregation he started in Thessalonica and urging them to "encourage each other and build each other up." So, you decide to tell your ministry team about your surprising early learning memory, including some of the unfortunate consequences to your self-image. You conclude by suggesting that "building each other up" should be a central goal of your congregation's educational ministry.

Indian actress Raashi Khanna aptly observes, "Genuine appreciation is rare to come by." Perhaps it is why a "strength bombardment exercise" is repeatedly the single, most valued activity by students in my interpersonal communication classes over the years. This activity centers on what we appreciate, like, respect, or admire about one another. Students write down several qualities (e.g., characteristics, traits, abilities, or strengths) they especially appreciate about each person. Then focusing on one person at a time, students take turns bombarding that person with the qualities they've written down.[1] These gifts of affirmation demonstrate how expressing appreciation builds each other up and helps raise our self-esteem. Such positive feedback results in gaining a more balanced and accurate view of ourselves.

In this chapter, you'll find six guidelines for learning how we can improve the way we express appreciation. Also, look for practical wisdom and best practices gleaned from recent research on how expressions of appreciation give us the power to transform our relationships for the better in our congregations and everyday lives.

Guidelines for Expressing Appreciation

1. Think of Appreciation as Powerful and Transformative Energy.

What comes to mind when you think of appreciation? Perhaps it is hearing someone say to you, "You just don't appreciate what I've done for you," or "You should show your appreciation for what you have and have been given." In other words, someone feels unappreciated, and you should feel guilty. Here, expressing appreciation is seen as a duty or an obligation for something you've received or to someone for what they've done for you. When you feel and express appreciation, you're doing just what is expected of you. And when you do not feel and express your appreciation as expected, you should feel ashamed for not doing so.

In contrast to appreciation-as-obligation is the more common understanding of appreciation-as-valuing. For example, land appreciates in value. It's worth increases. Here, expressing appreciation is seen as our response of loving or delighting in something important we've received or have been given. Indeed, "Delight is incomplete until it is expressed," notes C. S. Lewis. Social scientists Rollin McCraty and Doc Childre define

---

1. For more information about this activity, see Appendix C, "Strength Bombardment Exercise," in my publication, *Communication in the Church*, 163–64.

appreciation as an active feeling of thankfulness with an energetic quality that uplifts our energy and spirit.[2]

Similarly, clinical psychologists Noelle C. Nelson and Jeannine Lemare Calaba point out the powerful, transformative nature of feeling appreciated by someone and by showing our appreciation to others: "Your spirits soar! You feel that you are important to that person; you feel competent and happy. Well, you have the same effect on others when you show your appreciation. When you deliberately decide to appreciate people or things, you don't wish them harm and you don't do harm. Instead, you nurture, support, and love. As a result, they—and you—are transformed."[3] Here, we see appreciation-as-energy. And what gives appreciation the energy to transform lives? *Gratitude plus valuing*, say Nelson and Calaba, a combination they believe gives appreciation its power as transformative energy.

Most people think of gratitude when they use the word "appreciation," suggest Nelson and Calaba. They view gratitude as a receptive energy that engages the heart. We feel grateful, for example, for someone's help, or are pleased with someone's generosity or goodness to us. The valuing aspect of appreciation also engages our minds and brings a dynamic energy. When we value something or someone, we actively use our mind to think about why it matters to us and what it is worth to us.

Nelson and Calaba also point out that appreciation is a choice we make: "Consciously choosing to value the people and things in your life is what makes it possible for you to use appreciation *proactively*. You don't have to wait for something pleasing to happen in order to start valuing. You can choose to value someone or something before they have contributed anything at all to your life. The act of proactively valuing transforms gratitude from an after-the-fact expressing of feeling to a before-the-fact, deliberate engaging of energy. This is the energy of appreciation!"[4]

Benedictine monk, ecumenist, and experimental psychologist David Steindl-Rast points out that gratitude is related to thankfulness. However, there is an important distinction between the two: while we are grateful *for* something, we are thankful *to* someone. Steindl-Rast comments, "the verb that goes with gratitude is *thanking*. There is no action word for gratefulness; its dynamism is self-contained. Being grateful is a state;

---

2. McCraty and Childre, "The Grateful Heart," 231.
3. Nelson and Calaba, *The Power of Appreciation*, 2.
4. Nelson and Calaba, *The Power of Appreciation* 3.

thanking is an action."[5] As writer William Arthur Ward puts it, "Feeling gratitude, and not expressing it, is like wrapping a present and not giving it." For example, I may congratulate myself with a fist pump or an "alright" exclamation for the skill and perseverance it took to complete a ridiculously hard Sudoku puzzle. Feelings of frustration are transformed into feelings of elation by a challenging task well met.

Let's examine the transformative power of appreciate-as-energy a little more closely. Thus far, we've learned that appreciation that comes from the heart results in an attitude of gratitude. And appreciation that comes from the mind leads to valuing and results in an action of thankfulness, as gratitude-in-action. Here are some ways the energy of appreciation is powerful and can transform most any experience into one you value and are grateful for:

- To develop self-confidence without being selfish or self-centered
- To better cope with change or crisis
- To create healthier communication
- To take the high road when confronted with blame, resentment, revenge, or anger
- To have more fulfilling and meaningful relationships
- To become more open-minded, non-judgmental, cooperative, and generous
- To deal more effectively with problem-solving, conflict, resistance, and power
- To increase satisfaction and joy at work and at home
- To promote faster healing and a healthier lifestyle[6]

The next time you get into an argument with a friend or colleague, you'll have a choice about how to respond. If you decide to take a win-lose, competitive approach, defensiveness and blaming often get in the way of productive problem-solving. Communication breaks down as you talk past each other and end up frustrated or even angry with one another. It may even strain your relationship for a time.

---

5. Steindl-Rast, "Gratitude as Thankfulness and as Gratefulness," 286. For more information about gratitude per se, see Bass, *Grateful*.
6. Nelson and Calaba, *The Power of Appreciation*, 4.

EXPRESSING APPRECIATION

What would happen if you were to take a win-win, exploratory, cooperative approach? Instead of responding with some version of "I'm right-you're-wrong," you might say something along these lines: "I think I see where you're coming from. And I value your right to think differently than me. In fact, I can appreciate your reasoning. However, I'm seeing things differently and here's the reasoning behind the way I see things. See what you think."

Next, you might be sure you understand one another by checking your perception of each other's reasoning. "Let's be sure we understand each other's reasoning correctly so that we have a better appreciation of how we're coming to different conclusions" (and then paraphrase your understanding of each other's reasoning). Perhaps you'll even discover you are seeing two different though equally valuable sides of the same issue. Your appreciation for one another's reasoning might lead you to see that both viewpoints are important aspects of your topic of conversation. It enlarges your thinking about a topic about which you began with an argument and apparent disagreement. You may even still disagree with one another, but now you may more easily decide to agree to disagree and not get stuck in spiraling conversation that ends in frustration. You value one another's thinking instead of discounting or ignoring each other's perspectives. And you've created a healthier relationship in the process.

By approaching conflict believing that each other's point of view is legitimate, our urge to fight is dissipated. Our appreciation of one another's thinking leads to productive conversation. Moreover, this problem-solving approach works in our interpersonal conflicts as well as in our workplace disputes and our global confrontations. The more we appreciate one another despite our differences the more likely we are to experience peaceful and healthy relationships in our personal lives, congregations, communities, and the world.

Here's an example of how expressing appreciation can transform feelings of anger and resentment. As you approach an intersection and begin to slow down behind a line of cars waiting at a stoplight, your spouse sees that no one is in the next lane over and asks, "Why don't you pull over into the empty lane?" As you change lanes, you feel anger and resentment flare up toward your spouse, and you let him know it. In exasperation, you say, "I didn't want to pull over into that lane because I like to let people who want to turn at the intersection be free to do so." To which your spouse responds, "Oh, I was concerned that we're running late for our hair appointments and thought it would save us a little time. I now see why you didn't want to change lanes, and I do appreciate your willingness to do so." Feeling your anger and resentment begin to lessen, you go on to say, "Well, thank you for understanding why I didn't want to change lanes, and for appreciating my willingness to change the way I usually drive. I guess it is okay this time." In this instance, your spouse's understanding of and appreciation for your hesitancy to change lanes helps defuse your anger and transforms your resentment to the point where they are short-lived. In fact, in this instance they die down as fast as they flare up.

2. Be Aware That Unexpressed Appreciation is Costly.

"When not shown appreciation, it gets to you," comments American basketball player Kareem Abdul-Jabbar. As noted at the beginning of this chapter, we have a common and harmful tendency to receive negative feedback more often than positive feedback. McCraty and Childre call this natural tendency to focus on negative thoughts and emotions to a greater extent than neutral or positive ones a "negativity bias." They claim it even has a neurophysiological effect on us.[7] For example, they point out, "although most people definitively claim that they love, care, and appreciate, it might shock many to realize the large degree to which these feelings are merely assumed or acknowledged cognitively, far more than they are actually experienced in their feeling world."[8] They add, "In the absence of conscious efforts to engage, build, and sustain positive perceptions and emotions, we all too automatically fall prey to feelings such as irritation, anxiety, worry, frustration, judgmentalness, self-doubt, and blame."[9] Connecting the impact of repeatedly rehashing such negative feelings to our neural architecture, McCraty and Childre continue, "Many people do not realize the extent to which these habitual response patterns dominate their internal landscape, diluting and limiting positive emotional experience

---

7. McCraty and Childre, "The Grateful Heart," 241–42. Also noting that negative feedback has more emotional impact than positive feedback, and that negative information and events take longer to wear off than positive information and events, is Cameron in "Organizational Compassion," 430.

8. McCraty and Childre, "The Grateful Heart," 241.

9. McCraty and Childre, "The Grateful Heart," 241–42.

and eventually becoming so familiar that they become ingrained in one's sense of self-identity."[10]

As we might expect, our proclivity for negative thoughts and emotions is costly in terms of forfeiting such benefits of positive emotions as:

- Improvement to health
- Increased longevity
- Increased mental flexibility and creativity
- Facilitation of broad-minded coping and innovative problem solving
- Promoting helpfulness, generosity, and cooperation

Empirical research and clinical practice are also finding such benefits of appreciation as:

- Feeling more peaceful, alert, energetic, and enthusiastic
- Having less stress and more resilience
- Having better immune systems
- Dissolving old resentments
- Attracting new relationships
- Gaining self-esteem
- Being healthier (e.g., better digestion, lower heart rate and blood pressure)[11]

So, what can we do about our lack of appreciation? We can identify several appreciation skills and practices that will help us receive these benefits of appreciation.

3. Expressing Appreciation is a Skill to Learn and Practice.

It is important to realize that expressing appreciation is a skill that can be learned and practiced. To unleash the power of appreciation and to create a lifestyle of expressing appreciation, here are some steps to facilitate these transformations:

---

10. McCraty and Childre, "The Grateful Heart," 242.
11. Nelson and Calaba, *The Power of Appreciation*, xi–xii.

Step One: Choose What You Want to Transform

- Decide what you want and be specific
- Be sure your desire is realistic
- Make necessary adjustments

Step Two: Discover the Feelings Behind Your Desire

- Determine what value or meaning your desire has to you
- Explore the feelings your desire prompts
- Generate specific feelings of valuing and gratitude

Step Three: Weed Out Conflicting Thoughts and Beliefs

- Examine your thoughts about what you want, its availability, and your ability to get it
- Replace negative or obstructive beliefs with positive or action-oriented thinking
- Create affirmations to bolster your new thinking and beliefs

Step Four: Launch Your Energy of Appreciation

- Appreciate what you already have
- Launch your desire with focused, intense appreciation
- Clear out unnecessary worry, fear, or doubt that gets in your way

Step Five: Practice Your Appreciation

- Stay alert and track how your desire is unfolding
- Adjust to unforeseen circumstances and express your appreciation creatively
- Adopt an attitude of trust, hope, and expectation[12]

Let's see how to practice these appreciation skill-building steps to transform a failing relationship. Imagine that while you and your partner really do love each other, your partner has allowed distractions such as

12. Nelson and Calaba, *The Power of Appreciation*, 59–76.

watching TV, spending what you see as excessive time on the computer, and going out with friends lead you to feel resentful, lonely, and bored with your relationship. Your partner also seems to show little interest in having an intimate relationship with you. How can a surge of appreciation rekindle intimacy and warmth in your relationship?

Step One: Choose what you want to transform. First, you decide that you'd like you and your partner to spend more quality time together as a couple. Next, you identify specific, attainable ways to do so, including starting one or two new regular activities together, e.g., go walking aerobically several times a week, play a card game once a day, or go to a movie together once a week.

Step Two: Discover the feelings behind your desire to spend more time together. You discern what spending more time would mean to you and how it can change your life. For example, you might feel less taken for granted, lonely, and ignored and more secure, connected, and affectionate.

Step Three: Weed out conflicting thoughts and beliefs. You wonder if your partner really cares enough about you and your relationship to spend more time together. You think that perhaps it's too late to even try to revive your intimacy. To counter these doubts, you decide to reframe your expectation that nothing can change, or that opportunity has passed you by. You choose to believe instead that maybe it's not too late after all, and that it really is possible to rekindle your love. At least you see each other every day and have opportunities to spend more time together. Then you solidify your new beliefs by regularly reminding yourself that opportunity awaits, old habits can be replaced by new ones, and, since other people rekindle intimacy, so, too, can the two of you.

Step Four: Launch your energy of appreciation. You start by appreciating the meaningful ways you already spend together. You watch several TV programs together. You have most breakfasts and dinners together and share meal preparation and clean up chores. You do have mutual interests, including playing games and going to movies. You aren't nagging your partner and creating even more distance between the two of you. And you are grateful that your partner has accepted your invitation to go to a movie with you on a day off instead of going out to play tennis with a colleague yet again. Finally, you give yourself a ray of hope that you and your partner will hold hands during the movie and rekindle a little warmth in one another's presence.

Step Five: Practice your appreciation. You watch for small changes. You seize opportunities to talk about what is on TV. You change your schedule, so you are free when you partner has a day off. And you show your appreciation by surprising your partner with the suggestion of a favorite restaurant for dinner after the movie. You even offer to pay for your dinners—drinks and tip included. You also decide to go to a movie with a showtime that allows enough time for a relaxing meal and intimacy afterward.

You may adapt and use these skill-building, appreciation-as-energy best practices to transform similar challenges in your life, thereby increasing your own well-being as well as those in your sphere of influence. Whether it is coping with stress, overcoming communication breakdowns, or promoting human justice, be intentional about practicing these steps. You'll upgrade your appreciation skillset and increase the likelihood of making the changes you desire to enhance the quality of life and overall human flourishing for yourself, your congregation, and our global community.

4. Appreciation Matters.

"The deepest craving of human nature is the need to be appreciated." So says philosopher and psychologist William James. For example, the lack of appreciation we discussed earlier matters such that it is the primary reason most workers cite for leaving their jobs, as high as 79%.[13] Moreover, research finds that 66% of workers say they will leave their job if they feel unappreciated—and this number jumps to 76% for millennial employees.[14] In *The 5 Languages of Appreciation in the Workplace*, marriage and family counselor Gary Chapman, and psychologist Paul White, comment: "Something deep within the human psyche cries out for appreciation. When that need is unmet, then job satisfaction will be diminished."[15] They point out that when relationships are not nurtured by appreciation, there are predictable results such as:

- Team members experience a lack of connectedness with others and with the organization's mission
- Workers become discouraged, feeling there's always more to do and no one appreciates what they are doing

---

13. See Nordstrom, "79% of Employees Quit."
14. See Lipman, "66% Of Employees Would Quit."
15. Chapman and White, *The 5 Languages of Appreciation*, 15–16.

- Employees complain about their work, their colleagues, and their supervisor
- Team members eventually think seriously about leaving the organization and search for other employment[16]

Even as lack of appreciation has predictable results, so, too, does expressing appreciation. When workers were asked what most motivates them to do great work, being appreciated through recognition of their effort and achievements was three times more important than any other factor—more so than self-motivation, autonomy, promotion, or pay, especially for younger workers.[17] The primary reason appreciation and recognition motivate workers is that it engages them by increasing their sense of opportunity and feeling of well-being. Feeling appreciated also increases their work performance. For example, expressing appreciation by recognizing healthcare workers for great work increases the satisfaction of their patients.[18] Indeed, creating a culture of appreciation in the workplace increases worker satisfaction, innovation, trust, recruitment, and retention. And as we saw in chapter 1, we can even take a "gift-centered" approach to annual performance reviews rather than a "problem-centered" one. This type of asset-based job evaluation centers more on what we appreciate about our employees and less on what we don't like about or find lacking in their performance.

Organizational researchers and consultants David Sturt, Todd Nordstrom, Kevin Ames, and Gary Beckstrand call attention to three naturally-occurring opportunities for expressing appreciation in most organizations: encouraging effort, rewarding results, and celebrating careers.[19] They find that *encouraging effort* increases confidence in worker skills, lets workers know their work is on target, and improves relationships with their colleagues and leaders. Encouragement might include approval of creative efforts and resources along with the freedom to fail and try again. A shout-out in a team meeting, a phone call, and a handwritten note or email also can provide timely and personalized appreciation.

Rewarding results makes a difference by inspiring innovation, productivity, and performance; remembering achievements over time; and

---

16. Chapman and White, *The 5 Languages of Appreciation*, 22.
17. Sturt et al., *Appreciate*, 13–15.
18. Sturt et al., *Appreciate*, 17.
19. Sturt et al., *Appreciate*, 62.

boosting morale and pride in the organization. Rewards can include gifts, gift cards, and social media praise.

Celebrating career milestones encourages retention, creates company pride, and elevates achievement. Unique values, skills, and contributions are worth celebrating. Milestone expectations need to be clear, celebrations well planned, and invitations made to significant people within and outside the organization.

Research also indicates that those who express appreciation improve their own drive and determination, organizational connection, work relationships, and personal standing in their organization.[20]

In short, expressing appreciation through recognition inspires great work, increases engagement, encourages innovation and productivity, improves trust in leader-member relationships, and attracts and retains workers.

5. The Way We Express Appreciation Matters.

Chapman and White say that the way we express appreciation matters, too. Based on Chapman's pioneering work, *The 5 Love Languages*, they find that the best way to communicate appreciation varies from person to person. Therefore, they propose that we tailor the way we express appreciation using people's primary appreciation "language." Each of us wants to know that what we do makes a difference, is valued, and has impact. Appreciation has the power to transform our feelings of not making a difference to feelings of being valued for who we are and what we do. Words of appreciation are most meaningful to some people, while others more highly value physical touch, quality time, acts of service, or tangible gifts. Learn a person's favored language of appreciation by observing what they do for others, what they request of others, and what they complain about or hope will change.

Authentic *words of appreciation* should be communicated in the setting or context that is most meaningful. It may be a personal one-to-one affirmation for handling a difficult assignment, or positive feedback in front of others about someone's leadership excellence. Or it might be a hand-written letter or email complimenting someone's relational skills or important work accomplishment or giving special thanks publicly for an especially important contribution to the organization's success.

---

20. Sturt et al., *Appreciate*, 155.

EXPRESSING APPRECIATION

Communicating appreciation through appropriate and welcome *physical touch* can include a pat on the back for inspiration to persevere through a challenging task, a high five for a job well done, or a hug of support during times of duress.

Quality time means giving someone your focused attention. It may be expressing appreciation through asking about someone's well-being, sitting down and enjoying one another's presence, a check-in phone call or text message, and listening empathically to someone's challenging situation or creative idea.

Acts of service can include staying after hours to help someone complete a project, offering to complete a task that frees up someone's time for more important tasks, helping to solve someone's computer problem, or bringing food when someone is working late.

Tangible gifts from an employer, supervisor or co-worker might include a special gift card, tickets to a sporting or cultural event, leaving work early or getting some extra time off, or lodging for a mini vacation.

6. Use Appreciation to Make Positive Organizational Change.

Perhaps the most common attempt to transform people, organizations, and the world is through a deficit-based approach to fix or solve problems. This approach identifies what is wrong or lacking and seeks to find a solution to deal with the problem. A recent alternate way to bring about change is to use an asset-based approach that builds on what's best, gives life, and positive potential. Appreciative Inquiry (AI) is one such asset-based, affirmative, and cooperative search for the best in people, their organizations, and the world around them. As such, AI is a philosophy that uses an approach or a process (what's known as the 4-D Cycle of *Discovery, Dream, Design, and Destiny*) to engage people in making effective and positive change.[21] It assumes that all organizations have something that works right, gives it life, and has importance to its stakeholders. In short, AI connects what is positive in an organization to its vision, energy, and strategic plan to make the changes it seeks a reality.

AI defines "appreciate" as a verb, meaning to value something: "It's the act of recognizing the best in people or the world around us; to affirm the past and present strengths, successes and potentials; to perceive those things that give life (health, vitality, and excellence) to living systems. It also means

---

21. See Cooperrider et al., *Appreciative Inquiry Handbook*, xv.

to increase in value (e.g., the economy has appreciated in value). Synonyms: valuing, prizing, esteeming, and honoring."[22]

Consider that your congregation faces the task of finding a new pastor. A search committee is formed and creates a process to guide its work. Taking an AI approach, it decides to discover or re-discover what are your congregation's strengths on which to envision or base its dreams and attract a new pastor. After crafting what your congregation might become, the search committee decides what destiny can empower and sustain a positive future, and it describes their next pastor. In other words, based on your congregation's strengths or assets, the search committee creates a mission statement that sets the stage for drafting a position description that it can use to attract a new pastor to help your congregation live into its hopes for the future.

In the discovery phase, the search committee interviews selected leaders, groups, and members of your congregation using such questions as:

- What is a peak experience where you felt most alive and engaged in our congregation's ministry?
- What do you most value about yourself, your ministry, and our congregation?
- What core factors give life to our congregation without which we would cease to exist?
- What three wishes do you have for enhancing the health and vitality of our congregation?
- What key characteristics or competencies do you desire in our next pastor?

Next, the search committee visualizes a dream for the congregation based on the themes identified in the discovery phase and captures the dream in a narrative statement of its idealized future, including a description of a new pastor. It then reports back to the congregation's leaders, groups, and members and gets their feedback and buy in. Now it is ready to use the congregation's strengths and assets to create targets, goals, strategies, and action items to design a path for achieving its destiny and finding its pastor for the future.

---

22. Cooperrider et al., *Appreciative Inquiry Handbook*, 433.

Summary and Conclusion

Appreciation is sometimes viewed as a duty: appreciation-as-obligation. A more common and helpful perspective is to see appreciation as something to take delight in, appreciation-as-valuing. Appreciation is powerful. It is an energy that can make our spirits soar. Appreciation is a choice we make to be thankful. It is gratitude-in-action. And it has the capacity to transform our lives by developing self-confidence, coping with change, and overcoming resentment. It handles conflict, solves problems, and increases the joy of life. And, perhaps most importantly, it creates healthier communication, relationships, and lifestyles.

Unexpressed appreciation is costly in terms of the benefits of appreciation we forfeit. Fortunately, there are skills and practices we can learn to express appreciation. A five-step process for unleashing the power of appreciation is introduced and demonstrated.

Appreciation matters. It is one of our deepest cravings. It is a primary motivation for doing great work. Appreciation through recognition motivates workers by increasing their sense of opportunity and feeling of well-being. Encouraging effort, rewarding results, and celebrating career milestones are three naturally occurring ways to express appreciation in most organizations.

The way we express appreciation also matters. People respond to appreciation differently, so we need to learn their primary appreciation languages. We can communicate appreciation through authentic words, physical touch, quality time, acts of service, and tangible gifts.

Finally, appreciation can be used to foster positive changes in organizations. Appreciative Inquiry is an asset-based, affirmative, and cooperative process for bringing out the best in people, their organizations, and the world. It includes these four phases: discovery, dreaming, designing, and destiny.

This chapter's six guidelines offer practical wisdom and best practices for expressing appreciation that transform our relationships for the better in our congregations and everyday lives. Appreciation is a powerful way to enhance the quality of life and human flourishing for ourselves, our communities, and our world.

Practical Applications

1. What is your experience with negative bias, on the one hand, and positive feedback or affirmation, on the other hand? How about in your congregation's experience?

2. What impact has appreciation, or the lack of appreciation, had in your life? How about in your relationships and congregation?

3. In what ways has unexpressed appreciation been costly in your life, relationships, and congregation?

4. How can you improve your skills and practices of expressing appreciation? How about your congregation?

5. What is your primary motivation for doing great work? How effective has appreciation through recognition been used to encourage effort, reward results, and celebrate career milestones in your workplaces? How can a culture of appreciation be enhanced? How about in your congregation?

6. What is your primary appreciation language? How effective do you think most people are at detecting and using each other's appreciation languages? How can we become more effective in our lives and congregations?

7. How can Appreciative Inquiry be used to make positive changes in your congregation?

For Further Study

Bass, Diana Butler. *Grateful: The Transformative Power of Giving Thanks* (New York: HarperOne, 2018).

Chapman, Gary D., and Paul E. White. *The 5 Languages of Appreciation in the Workplace: Empowering Organizations by Encouraging People*, rev. and updated (Chicago: Northfield, 2012).

Cooperrider, David L., Diana Whitney, and Jacqueline M. Stavros. *Appreciative Inquiry Handbook: For Leaders of Change*, 2nd ed. (Brunswick, OH: Crown Custom, 2008).

Emmons, Robert A., and Michael E. McCullough, eds. *The Psychology of Gratitude* (New York: Oxford University Press, 2004).

Nelson, Noelle C., and Jeannine Lemare Calaba. *The Power of Appreciation: The Key to a Vibrant Life* (Hillsboro, OR: Beyond Books, 2003).

Sturt, David, Todd Nordstrom, Keven Ames, and Gary Backstrand. *Appreciate: Celebrating People, Inspiring Greatness* (Salt Lake City, UT: O.C. Tanner Institute, 2017).

Chapter 6

Doing Justice

Injustice anywhere is a threat to justice everywhere.
—Martin Luther King Jr.

Seek justice, rescue the oppressed.—Isaiah 1:17

Religious leaders decide to protest a decision by their county council to cut human services from the county budget. The county is projecting a huge budget deficit and seeks to get its budget under control. A clergy spokesperson attends a budget hearing and presents their concerns to council members. They view the council's projected social service budget cuts as an injustice against the county's most vulnerable citizens: the poor, homeless, immigrants, elderly, youth, and children. Budget cuts include funding for essential childcare services as well as services for victims of domestic violence. Such projected budget cuts violate the community's values and responsibility to care for its most vulnerable citizens, rather than abandon them, argues the clergy spokesperson. Examples of caring for needy citizens by the congregations are cited, including provision of food, electric bill assistance, rental assistance, and homeless services. Congregations can serve the needs of citizens who fall through the cracks in the social service system but cannot fund primary social services. The spokesperson asks the county to restore essential social service funding and work with the faith communities in caring for the county's most vulnerable citizens.

The following day the County Executive contacts the clergy spokesperson and asks her to serve on a task force that will address the county's human services funding dilemma. Council members agree that providing for its most vulnerable citizens is a justice issue and decide that the county must continue funding its share of essential social services for all its citizens.

Here's another scenario about doing social justice, this time in our court systems. American politician and popular New York mayor Fiorello La Guardia faced a quandary while presiding at a police court. As recorded by journalist Bennett Cert, "one bitter cold day they brought a trembling old man before him, charged with stealing a loaf of bread. His family, he said, was starving. 'I've got to punish you,' declared La Guardia. 'The law makes no exception. I can do nothing but sentence you to a fine of ten dollars.'"[1] Faced with the seeming unfairness and harshness of such cold-hearted legal justice, La Guardia felt moved to take further action. But what could he do to make things right?

Here's the rest of the story: "[La Guardia] was reaching into his pocket as he added, 'Well, here's the ten dollars to pay your fine. And now I remit the fine.' He tossed a ten-dollar bill into his famous sombrero. 'Furthermore,' he declared, 'I'm going to fine everybody in this courtroom fifty cents for living in a town where a man has to steal bread in order to eat. Mr. Bailiff, collect the fines and give them to the defendant!' The hat was passed and an incredulous old man, with a light of heaven in his eyes, left the courtroom with a stake of forty-seven dollars and fifty cents."[2]

At one level, La Guardia had no choice but to fine the man for his crime. But what type of justice forces a man with nothing to pay a $10 fine? So, La Guardia pays the fine himself. However, seeing a bigger kind of injustice, and moved by empathy, compassion, and kind-heartedness, La Guardia draws on simple social justice to create a seemingly fair way to make things right. And perhaps most astonishing, this going-the-extra-mile search for some type of alternative justice appears to be a feel-good, right-sounding thing to do. It is what the prophet Isaiah is getting at: "Seek justice, rescue the oppressed."

Not all community protests, funding hearings, and courtroom experiences will turn out the way these scenarios did, nor should they. However, they point the way toward doing justice in our communities, toward fairness in human relationships, and toward making things right that we all seek. In this chapter, you'll find five guidelines of practical wisdom for making things right when they go awry at home, at work, and in society. Also, look for best practices gleaned from recent research for how doing justice has the power to transform your relationships for the better in your congregation and everyday life.

1. Fadiman, *The Little, Brown Book of Anecdotes*, 339.
2. Fadiman, *The Little, Brown Book of Anecdotes*, 339.

Guidelines for Doing Justice

1. Think of Justice as Centered in Relationships.

From the time we are small children, most of us have an innate sense of justice. We have a keen sensitivity for what is right and fair, and let other people know when they cross or violate our shared obligations to behave justly. This is what happened initially in the courtroom scenario. Indeed, fairness in keeping obligations is central to our individual sense of justice. Social justice, on the other hand, usually refers to obligations of citizens for the common good. It is what happened eventually in the county council scenario. As attorney and political analyst Angela Rye puts it, "I grew up always thinking that fighting for justice was our obligation, whether that's giving your voice to something, serving as a verbal advocate for someone, or physically being in spaces or occupying space to make and create change."

Ethicist Daniel Maguire suggests that the goal of social justice is to create a society where no one lacks their essential needs.[3] This pursuit is what led the county council to finally accept its social service fiscal responsibilities. And it is what moved La Guardia to go beyond the obligations of legal justice. Social work professor Frederic G. Reamer comments, "In the broadest sense, social justice refers to the fair allocation of human rights, protections, opportunities, obligations, and social benefits. Social justice also entails acknowledging and addressing social and economic inequalities, and seeking to eliminate discrimination and oppression associated with race, ethnicity, national origin, color, sex, sexual orientation, gender identity or expression, age, marital status, political belief, immigration status, and mental or physical disability."[4] This form of justice is often referred to as distributive justice and is our primary interest. A related type of justice, procedural justice, focuses on fairness in the way distribution decisions are made and implemented and will also be of interest. Other types of justice, and of lesser interest, include criminal or retributive justice, and restorative justice. Here the focus is on punishment for harm or wrongdoing and on restoring just relations among victims, offenders, and the community. For the most part, punishment for wrongdoing and the criminal justice system fall outside the scope of our interests in social justice.[5]

3. Maguire, "Religious Influences on Justice Theory," 33.
4. Reamer, "Social Justice and Criminal Justice," 269–70.
5. For more information on retributive and restorative justice, see the following: Sullivan and Tifft, *Handbook of Restorative Justice,* and Johnstone and Van Ness,

Justice, though, is more than keeping or violating social norms or obligations. At its roots, justice is about how we treat one another. Ultimately, this is what made the difference in our county council and courtroom scenarios. The relationship between religious leaders and council members was transformed from antagonists to partners for social justice. They agreed to care enough about treating vulnerable citizens responsibly that eventually things were made right fiscally. And the relationship between La Guardia and the old man was transformed from the constraints of individual justice to the imperative of social justice. La Guardia cared enough about treating the man fairly that he made things right in the long run. Here is how theological educator Chris Marshall puts it: "Justice is all about relationships."[6] Calling justice comprehensively relational, Marshall continues: "It [justice] is not a private attribute that an individual has on his or her own, independent of anyone else. Nor is it a set of abstract norms about balance or equity or fairness. Justice means doing all that is necessary to create and sustain healthy, constant, and life-giving relationships between persons. Justice is to be measured by the extent to which people honor their obligations to live in relationships that uphold the equal dignity and rights of the other. Both elements are important—relationships that are wholesome, and faithfulness to the demands of such relationships by all parties involved."[7]

Justice is not without paradox, however. For example, justice is both impartial, and partial. It is impartial when dealing with laws and regulations—everyone must be treated the same way. Justice in the courtroom is egalitarian. For example, there's no room for distorting justice, nor for accepting bribes. There is no room for undue privilege. Everyone is to be treated equally in the administration of legal justice. Procedural justice, on the other hand, deals with the way wealth, resources, opportunity, and power are distributed. Here partiality is necessary—a special concern or bias must be shown to vulnerable or disadvantaged groups and individuals such as widows, orphans, resident aliens, and the poor. Our courtroom scenario demonstrates this paradoxical nature of justice. It helps us understand why Mayor La Guardia faced a quandary in his courtroom.

Handbook of Restorative Justice. Also see Zehr, *The Little Book of Restorative Justice*; Johnstone, *A Restorative Justice Reader*; van Wormer and Walker, *Restorative Justice Today*; Umbreit and Peterson, *Restorative Justice Dialogue*; Zehr and Toews, *Critical Issues in Restorative Justice*; McLaughlin et al., *Restorative Justice*; and Marshall, *Beyond Retribution*.

6. Marshall, *The Little Book of Biblical Justice*, 35.
7. Marshall, *The Little Book of Biblical Justice*, 35–36.

The Universal Declaration of Human Rights[8] is perhaps the most comprehensive and global statement about and commitment to a socially just world. Its 30 Articles center on the provision of essential needs for all people, and on the protection of vulnerable, marginalized, and disadvantaged groups and individuals from oppression, discrimination, and exclusion. Written in the context of global economic depression, genocide, two world wars, and the dismantling of colonial empires, it is based on these five social justice principles:

- Human dignity (Article 1)
- Non-discrimination (Article 2)
- Civil and political rights (Articles 3-21)
- Economic, social, and cultural rights (Articles 22-27)
- Solidarity rights (Articles 28-30)[9]

Especially important for our interests in doing justice are such rights as:

- Equality and non-discrimination
- Life, liberty, and personal security
- Property ownership
- Social security
- Desirable work
- Adequate living standard
- Education
- Rest and leisure[10]

From our discussion thus far, it is apparent that doing justice includes:

- Values, e.g., caring, democracy, fairness, participation,[11] individual dignity and worth

---

8. See the Universal Declaration of Human Rights, at https://www.un.org/en/universal-declaration-human-rights/

9. See Wronka, "Human Rights," 219–20.

10. For a related list of capabilities all citizens need to achieve what they want to do and be for their welfare and well-being in a just society, see Kim and Sherraden, "The Capability Approach," 208.

11. Social justice feminism makes parity of participation a central value, and emphasizes strategies of redistribution, recognition, and representation. For more information,

- Objectives, e.g., reduce inequalities and increase inclusion aimed at structural change and systemic transformation
- Policies, e.g., political, social, economic, and environmental
- Practices, e.g., redistribute resources and dismantle oppression and undue privilege[12]

Since doing justice includes righting what has gone wrong and restoring things to a condition of rightness, we need to consider two related components of justice: punishment and mercy. Clearly, justice tilts towards restoration, rather than retribution. The place of punishment is to deter wrongdoing, to be accountable and take responsibility, and to help bring about restitution and restoration. We often think of mercy and justice in opposition to one another, wherein mercy may suspend or disregard the penalty that justice requires. From a strictly legal standpoint, this view of mercy may even be perceived as resulting in injustice. However, it is Abraham Lincoln who said, "I have always found that mercy bears richer fruits than strict justice." From a relational perspective, mercy can help restore healthy relationships rather than interfere with justice. No one is perfect; indeed, everyone is guilty of wrongdoing. Consequently, as Marshall points out, "compassionate acceptance of human fallibility is essential to the functioning of healthy relationships. Where failure occurs, justice must be seasoned with mercy, or it is not true justice."[13]

When we return to the Judeo-Christian trilogy of doing justice, loving kindness, and walking humbly with your God, we now come to the notions of making things right, and of restoring or securing abundant life for everyone. As theologian Walter Brueggemann points out, "Justice is to sort out what belongs to whom, and to return it to them."[14] It is concerned with who benefits and who is harmed. It means courageously challenging and radically changing social systems of haves and have-nots. Suggests Brueggemann, it means a radical reordering of social relationships involving *entitlements* to protect the weak against the strong; *debt cancellation* to permit the disenfranchised to resume their place of power, respect, and dignity; and *land redistribution* to return property to its rightful owner so that all may flourish.

---

see Gray et al., "Social Justice Feminism," 173–187.

12. See Fook, "Social Justice and Critical Theory," 161, 171.

13. Marshall, *The Little Book of Biblical Justice*, 37.

14. Brueggemann, "Voices of the Night," 5.

Reparations precede reconciliation, as professor of religion Jennifer Harvey suggests in *Dear White Christians: For Those Still Longing for Racial Reconciliation*. She comments: "It is time to begin (in some cases, again) the work of reparations as our fundamental and formative approach to the multiracial work of pursuing racial justice both with and beyond the church."[15]

When justice calls for reallocating social goods and power, those who have more than their fair share commonly seek to defend their unjust position, power, and resources. Greed, self-righteousness, fear, anger, rage, and hatred often lead to acts of vengeance such as abuse, terror, and war. Remember, though, Helen Keller's counsel: "Until the great mass of the people shall be filled with the sense of responsibility for each other's welfare, social justice can never be attained." Or, as Martin Luther King Jr. puts it: "Injustice anywhere is a threat to justice everywhere." Cessation of violence, liberation from unjust social systems, and the transformation of unhealthy relationships are possible through such practices as humility and empathy, compassion and kindness, forgiveness and trust, and appreciation.

Consider our neighbors without adequate housing. Our other-centered political humility can lead us to an awareness of our city government's struggle to develop effective funding strategies for emergency, transitional, and permanent housing. Our experience of empathy for the human suffering of vulnerable, marginalized, and disadvantages neighbors, especially those with substance abuse and mental illness, can stir up feelings of compassion for them and move us to acts of kindness such as volunteering at homeless shelters and food pantries. Then too, the relationships we build with homeless families over supper provided by our congregations may give us opportunity to ask their forgiveness for years of indifference to their struggles. And our appreciation for the nuances of governmental priorities and policies means we make long-range, realistic commitments for achieving social justice goals and objectives. Finally, our trust in the power of government to make a difference gives us and our congregations the patient persistence to shape public opinion and social structures by advocating for social justice practices, capabilities, and opportunities for homeless neighbors at town-hall meetings. For example, when our county council holds its next budget hearings on social service spending, we can monitor funding proposals for homelessness and voice our support for such expenditures.

---

15. Harvey, *Dear White Christians*, xix.

2. Poverty and Economic Inequality Undermine Justice.

Sociologist Mark Rank presents compelling evidence that economic inequality and poverty distort and undermine our sense and practice of doing justice. He points out that these conditions undercut our commitments to fairness and justice: "They erode the idea that all citizens have full access and entitlement to certain rights, they damage the principal of equality of opportunity, and they create conditions that are neither deserved nor in balance with prior actions."[16] And he suggests that the best measure of a just society is by the way it treats those who are poorest and most vulnerable. As Albert Einstein comments, "Striving for social justice is the most valuable thing to do in life."

Citing overwhelming evidence that justice in America tilts heavily in favor of the well-off rather than the needy, even more so than in other wealthy countries, Rank issues this challenge: "It is time for us to awake from the 40 years of slumber that has been going on."[17] Perhaps Sheryl Crow is right: "Justice is a fading light." Rank continues, "It is time to venture down a new road, to a country where not just some children, but every American child receives a first rate education. We need to create a country where if you work full-time, you won't have to worry that your family will still be living in poverty; a country where democracy is not simply a hostage to the highest bidders; and a country where we respect and take to heart the principles, not of liberty and justice for some, but of liberty and justice for all."[18]

While poverty and economic inequality are serious social justice challenges, all is not bleak or hopeless. For example, global health expert Hans Rosling points out that while extreme poverty is one of the global risks we should worry about, the proportion of the world's population living in extreme poverty has almost halved in the last twenty years.[19] Moreover, more than three-quarters of the world's population now lives in middle-income countries, nine percent in high-income countries, and only sixteen percent in low-income countries.[20] And yet, even though

---

16. Rank, "Why Poverty and Inequality Undermine Justice," 444.
17. Rank, "Why Poverty and Inequality Undermine Justice," 445.
18. Rank, "Why Poverty and Inequality Undermine Justice," 445.
19. See Rosling et al., *Factfulness*, 277.
20. Rosling et al., *Factfulness*, 3, 277.

eight hundred million people worldwide still suffer in extreme poverty, Rosling offers this hopeful prospect:

> We also know the solutions: peace, schooling, universal basic health care, electricity, clean water, toilets, contraceptives, and microcredits to get market forces started. There's no innovation needed to end poverty. It's all about walking the last mile with what's worked everywhere else. And we know that the quicker we act, the smaller the problem, because as long as people remain in extreme poverty they keep having large families and their numbers keep increasing. Providing these necessities of a decent life, quickly, to the final billion is a clear, fact-based priority.[21]

Even terrorism is often rooted in perceived injustice, as American political activist Jodie Evans suggests: "What causes terrorism is disrespect, a lack of justice, and poverty." And Coretta Scott King's words bear repeating here: "we can prevent many people from becoming terrorists by truly listening to people who feel they've been treated unjustly and responding to their concerns with a sense of justice and compassion."

3. Use the Arts to Promote Social Justice.

While the arts are useful for our enjoyment, education, and entertainment, they also can make profound contributions to advancing social justice agendas, movements, and change. For example, they can promote efforts to eliminate the oppression and domination of exploited, marginalize, and powerless people and groups. Here are some of the ways such arts as literature, music, digital video, and cinema can promote social justice:

- Raise consciousness and awareness
- Create dialogue
- Give voice and tell stories to make the invisible visible
- Work towards equity and justice
- Foster individual empowerment and participation
- Bring people together and build relationships among individuals and groups

---

21. Rosling et al., *Factfulness*, 240–41.

- Create new visions and open new imaginations for what the world could be[22]

My initial awakening about racism came through reading such books as *Soul on Ice* by Eldridge Cleaver and *Black Like Me* by John Howard Griffin. Movies starring Sydney Poitier such as *Guess Who's Coming to Dinner* and *For Love of Ivy* raised my consciousness about racial equality and relationships. My awakening led to conversations about racism with my parents that heretofore had never happened. I discovered that many towns in my State of Oregon still had racist laws preventing people of color from staying overnight. The folk music of singers such as Joan Baez and Peter, Paul, and Mary, resonated with my evolving passion for human justice as did my study of liberation theology.

More recently, I facilitated an adult education class about facing intolerance and promoting diversity using a DVD series, *Embracing Interfaith Cooperation: Eboo Patel on Coming Together to Change the World*. Inspired by his faith as a Muslim, his Indian heritage, and his American citizenship, Patel offers a vision of interfaith harmony and presents religion as a bridge of cooperation rather than a barrier of division. I've also recently engaged in dialogue about of the pervasiveness of white privilege with members of a study group after reading such books as *Understanding White Privilege: Creating Pathways to Authentic Relationships Across Race* by Frances E. Kendall and *Waking Up White and Finding Myself in the Story of Race* by Debby Irving. Likewise, our study group's primer on the dynamics of power was Walter Wink's *The Powers That Be: Theology for a New Millennium*. And our conversations about *Always with Us? What Jesus Really Said about the Poor* by Liz Theoharis helped us envision a world without poverty and take steps to use our privilege in helping to end poverty.[23] As Pulitzer Prize-winning American journalist Isabel Wilkerson puts it in *Caste: The Origins of Our Discontents*, "The price of privilege is the moral duty to act when one sees another person treated unfairly."[24] Books on my current reading list include *America's Unholy Ghosts: The Racist Roots of Our Faith and Politics* by Joel Edward Goza, *How to Be an*

---

22. Sakamoto, "The Use of the Arts in Promoting Social Justice," 464.

23. For more information about the use of literature, music, and cinema to promote social justice, see Clarke, "By Its Absence: Literature and the Attainment of Social Justice Consciousness," 480–91; Taylor, "Music and Social Justice," 492–501; and Sim, "Social Justice and Cinema," 502–12.

24. Wilkerson, *Caste*, 386.

Antiracist by Ibram X. Kendi, and *White Fragility: Why It's So Hard for White People to Talk About Racism* by Robin DiAngelo.

4. Environmental Justice is Elusive.

"The trends that are shaping the twenty-first-century world embody both promise and peril. Globalization, for example, has lifted hundreds of millions of people out of poverty while contributing to social fragmentation and a massive increase in inequality, not to mention serious environmental damage."[25] So says German engineer, economist, and business policy professor Klaus Martin Schwab. Indeed, we're living at a time when our planet faces multiple challenges, not the least of which are environmental challenges.

First, though, as we turn to the topic of environmental justice, we need a working definition. One definition refers to the disproportionately high and averse human health or environmental effects on minority populations and low-income populations.[26] Strategies to achieve environmental justice may include:

- Identifying and addressing disproportionately high and adverse human health or environmental effects of government programs, policies, and activities on minority populations and low-income populations
- Promoting enforcement of all health and environmental statutes in areas with minority or low-income populations
- Improving research and data collection relating to the health and environment of minority and low-income populations
- Identifying differential patterns of consumption of natural resources among minority and low-income populations
- Ensuring greater public participation[27]

Another way to view environmental justice is "the fair treatment and meaningful involvement of all people regardless of race, color, national origin, or income with respect to the development, implementation, and

---

25. From brainyquote.com.
26. Kuehn, "Environmental Justice," 320.
27. Kuehn, "Environmental Justice," 320.

enforcement of environmental laws, regulations, and policies."[28] Included in this broader understanding of environmental justice are such outcomes as:

- Cessation of the production of all toxins, hazardous wastes, and radioactive materials
- Rights to political, economic, cultural, and environmental self-determination of all peoples
- Accountability of all waste producers for damages, including compensation and reparations for victims of environmental injustice
- Rights of citizens to participate as equal partners at every level of decision-making
- Rights of all workers to a safe and healthy work environment
- Recognition that governmental acts of environmental injustice are violations of international law
- Recognition of the special legal and governmental relationship of Native Peoples[29]

Empirical research shows disproportionate public health and environmental risks for poor and marginalized individuals and societies. For example, scholars conclude that the impact of climate change are most serious on people from the poorest nations.[30] Even more disconcerting is the now well-established link between wealthier countries as the primary cause of climate change and poorer nations as the most exposed and vulnerable to the adverse effects of climate change. Consequently, environmental costs are greater for poorer nations while people in wealthier nations enjoy a greater amount of benefits from these costs. So, global climate change is a distributive justice concern.

These unequal environmental exposures and benefits are also evident in the United States by race, ethnicity, and economic class. This inequity is true, for example, in that exposure to harmful pesticides, toxic air pollution, greenhouse gas emissions, sewer and storm water drainage, unclean water systems, and hazardous waste sites is greatest for people of color and lower-income communities. Indian tribes are especially adversely impacted by nuclear weapons testing, mining, and hazardous waste disposal sites. Besides

---

28. Kuehn, "Environmental Justice," 320.
29. Kuehn, "Environmental Justice," 320–21.
30. Kuehn, "Environmental Justice," 324.

harm to public health and natural resources, tribes and their members enjoy little direct benefit from environmental protections.[31]

The unjust distribution of environmental threats, costs, and benefits even extends to such quality of life impacts as fires, traffic congestion, neighborhood park locations, and decreased property values.[32]

Sadly, solutions for addressing these environmental inequities and inequalities are elusive and uncommon. Proposals range from doing nothing, to offering compensation to affected people and communities, to banning activities that exacerbate the disparities. Nonetheless, as environmental legal scholar Robert Kuehn concludes, "the inability to find consensus for defining or resolving allegations of distributive injustice does not make the claims of affected communities any less legitimate or the evidence of distributive inequities any less compelling. It does mean that until governments confront these political and legal issues, instances of distributive injustice are likely to go unresolved."[33] A rather bleak prospect, indeed.

While distributive environmental injustice is pervasive and solutions elusive, let's look at the role and impact of environmental policies and procedures. American professor of law and philosophy Ronald Dworkin defines procedural justice as "the right to treatment as an equal. This is the right, not to an equal distribution of some good or opportunity, but the right to equal concern and respect in the political decision about how these goods and opportunities are to be distributed."[34] No less than the Greek philosopher Aristotle was an advocate of "equal sharing in ruling and being ruled." Our focus here is on political and participative fairness in decision-making and implementation. An example of exercising procedural justice is governmental environment agencies being directed to ensure participation and access to information by ethnic minority and low-income individuals and groups. Other examples include demands that public policy is based on mutual respect and justice for all people, is free from bias or discrimination, includes participation as equal partners in decision-making, and results in fair implementation and outcomes.

Unfortunately, procedural justice for people of color and lower-income communities is as elusive as it is with distributive justice. According to research, people of color and lower-income:

31. Kuehn, "Environmental Justice," 324–25.
32. Kuehn, "Environmental Justice," 325.
33. Kuehn, "Environmental Justice," 325.
34. Dworkin, *Taking Rights Seriously*, 273.

- Are not well represented by interest groups lobbying and litigating before governmental authorities on environmental protection issues
- Are underrepresented in government agencies responsible for environmental processes
- While overexposed to environmental risks are underrepresented in environmental policy-making agencies and commissions
- Lack technical, legal, and other resources to participate effectively in environmental decision-making processes
- Have little political influence over officials that make environmental decisions
- Lack public notice and convenient meeting times and places for environmental agency meetings
- Experience discrimination in environmental permitting and hearing processes
- Receive unfair treatment in the development and enforcement of environmental laws, regulations, and policies
- Are underrepresented in environmental impact studies, statements, and agreements[35]

Why, though, even where equitable environmental policies and protections are in place, do we not see greater evidence of procedural justice equity? Perhaps American environmental activist and law professor Robert F. Kennedy, Jr. is correct when he observes, "We have very strong environmental laws in the United States and elsewhere around the world. The problem is that they're seldom enforced."

Surely strong enforcement and corrective efforts are essential to ensure positive environmental justice outcomes. Nonetheless, renewed resolve, commitment, and actions are required to correct a huge array of other environmental procedural and distributional injustices that persist. Chinese environmental journalist Ma Jun suggests that the real barrier to solving China's environmental problems is neither lack of technology nor money, but lack of motivation and public education. He also offers this assessment of his country's environmental prospects when he comments, "Even the government understands that the environmental challenge is so big that no single agency can handle it. It needs collaboration among all the stakeholders—companies,

---

35. Kuehn, "Environmental Justice," 326–31.

governments, NCOs and the public. Public accountability will be the ultimate driving force."[36] California environmentalist and philanthropist Tom Steyer points out that his state has taken this approach to climate change and clean energy with positive outcomes. It has done so by building a coalition that includes community and environmental leaders, working families, unions, businesses, and communities of color.

No doubt it will also help to adopt the perspective of South Korean politician, diplomat, and former United Nations Secretary-General Ban Ki-moon, wherein he links environmental concerns to other social justice issues: "Saving our planet, lifting people out of poverty, advancing economic growth . . . these are one and the same fight. We must connect the dots between climate change, water scarcity, energy shortages, global health, food security and women's empowerment. Solutions to one problem must be solutions for all."[37] Likewise, T.V. personality Ellen DeGeneres suggest that we take yet another wholistic approach to facing our environmental challenges when she comments, "There's got to be a very powerful energy to fight [environmental destruction]. I think we need more love in the world. We need more kindness, more compassion, more joy, more laughter. I definitely want to contribute to that." Indeed, we and our congregations must develop such practices and relationships with others if we are to transform persistent and elusive environmental injustices into the realities of environmental justice.

5. Global Health Equity is Achievable.

Health inequities are a social injustice that is killing people on a grand scale. This alarming assessment comes from the World Health Organization's Commission on Social Determinants of Health.[38] The World Health Organization considers health inequities as unfair, avoidable, and remediable differences in health status between countries and between different groups of people within the same country. First, though, let's not overlook significant progress in overall world health. Life expectancy worldwide is seventy-two years of age. Undernourishment has plummeted as have new HIV infections and death from crimes. The rate of child immunization

36. From brainyquote.com.

37. From brainyquote.com.

38. See World Health Organization press release, "Inequities Are Killing People on Grand Scale."

worldwide is now eighty-eight percent, child cancer survival at eighty percent, and safe water at eighty-eight percent. And while life expectancy in low-income counties is only sixty-two years of age, most people have enough food to eat and access to improved water, most children are vaccinated, and most girls finish primary school.[39] We also learned earlier that only sixteen percent of the world's population now live in low-income countries, and that the proportion of people living in extreme poverty is about half of what it was twenty years ago.

Nonetheless, significant health inequities are found when comparing health indicators between richer and poorer nations, and between socioeconomic class within each nation. Risks for disease, ill-health, and death are significantly higher in poor nations and among people in lower socioeconomic classes. And this pattern persists over time and place.[40]

Even as health inequities are alarming and persistent, so also is global health equity achievable within a generation. So concludes the World Health Organization's 2008 Commission on Social Determinants of Health 250-page report, "Closing the Gap in a Generation: Health Equity Through Action on Social Determinants of Health."[41] Because the Commission believes social justice is a matter of life and death, it calls for urgent action. And it makes this bold aspirational assertion: "It is essential that governments, civil society, the World Health Organization, and other global organizations now come together in taking action to improve the lives of the world's citizens. Achieving health equity within a generation is achievable, it is the right thing to do, and now is the right time to do it."[42]

The Commission makes the following three overarching recommendations for achieving global health equity:

- Improve daily living conditions
- Tackle the inequitable distribution of power, money, and resources
- Measure and understand the problem and assess the impact of action[43]

Specific action areas include:

- Equitable start in life

---

39. For information about these statistics, see Rosling et al., *Factfulness*, 29–64.
40. Fritzell, "Health Inequality and Social Justice," 340.
41. World Health Organization, "Closing the Gap," 248.
42. World Health Organization, "Closing the Gap," iii.
43. World Health Organization, "Closing the Gap," 202, 204, 206.

- Healthy places for healthy people
- Fair employment and decent work
- Life-long income security
- Universal health care
- Health equity in policies, systems, and programs
- Fair financing
- Market responsibility
- Gender equity
- Political empowerment
- Health equity monitoring, training, and research[44]

Detailed recommendations are identified for each action area.

Ambitious milestones towards achieving health equity were established beginning in 2008 and continuing through 2040.[45] Significant accomplishments to date include all 194 UN member states endorsing the Rio Political Declaration on Social Determinants of Health in 2011. This declaration centers on these five action areas:

- To adopt better governance for health and development
- To promote participation in policy-making and implementation
- To further reorient the health sector towards reducing health inequities
- To strengthen global governance and collaboration
- To monitor progress and increase accountability[46]

Pledges of specific actions to be taken are outlined. Implementation of these actions since 2011 have strengthened human rights frameworks, extended universal health coverage, increased social and environmental health equity policies and programs, and improved monitoring systems for health equity progress.[47] Then in 2015 at the 70th session of the United Nations General Assembly, a new social, economic, and environmental development framework for 2016-2030 was adopted. In this resolution,

---

44. World Health Organization, "Closing the Gap," 202-206.
45. World Health Organization, "Closing the Gap," 198.
46. World Conference on Social Determinants of Health, "Rio Political Declaration."
47. World Health Organization, "Global Monitoring of Action."

"2030 Sustainable Development Agenda," member nations pledged to reduce inequalities across seventeen sustainable development goals and to "leave no one behind."[48] Included are the following sustainable development goals relating to health equity:

- End poverty in all its forms everywhere
- End hunger, achieve food security, and promote sustainable agriculture
- Ensure healthy lives and promote well-being for all at all ages
- Ensure equitable quality education, including lifelong learning opportunities for all
- Achieve gender equality and empower all women and girls
- Ensure availability and sustainable management of water and sanitation for all
- Ensure access to affordable, reliable, sustainable, and modern energy for all
- Ensure sustainable economic growth, productive employment, and decent work for all
- Reduce inequality within and among countries
- Make cities and human settlements inclusive, safe, resilient, and sustainable
- Ensure sustainable consumption and production patterns
- Promote peaceful, inclusive societies and provide access to justice for all
- Strengthen the means of implementation and revitalize global partnerships[49]

Specific actions and targets are also included in the resolution. Stakeholders identified are all governments and parliaments, the United Nations system and other international institutions, local authorities, indigenous peoples, civil society, business and the private sector, the scientific and academic community—in other words, *all people*. Hopefully, unaffected sideline observers will become enthusiastic environmental activists. The resolution declares,

---

48. United Nations General Assembly Resolution, "Transforming Our World."
49. United Nations General Assembly Resolution, "Transforming Our World," 14.

DOING JUSTICE

> Millions have already engaged with, and will own, this Agenda. It is an Agenda of the people, by the people and for the people—and this, we believe, will ensure its success. The future of humanity and of our planet lies in our hands. It lies also in the hand of today's younger generation who will pass the torch to future generations. We have mapped the road to sustainable development; it will be for all of us to ensure that the journey is successful and its gains irreversible.[50]

Benjamin Franklin's admonition has perhaps been neither more apt nor urgent: "Justice will not be served until those who are unaffected are as outraged as those who are."

The Presbyterian Church (U.S.A.) has created a helpful study and devotional guide for achieving the seventeen sustainable development goals.[51] Useful for individuals and groups this resource gives a snapshot of each goal, some of their targets, and ways the denomination and its global partners are working to achieve the sustainable development agenda. Here is a note to readers from this resource:

> As we at the Presbyterian Ministry at the United Nations of the Presbyterian Church (U.S.A.) started examining the Goals and their targets for achievement, we realized that this is work that the Church has been engaged in for centuries. From eradication of hunger and poverty to treating the earth with respect, our church has been working to achieve these Goals since before their existence![52]

Here are some specific actions "we the people" can take to accomplish the goal, "to ensure healthy lives and promote well-being for all at all ages," by 2030:

- Reduce global maternal mortality
- End preventable deaths of newborns and children
- End the epidemics of AIDS, tuberculosis, malaria, and other communicable diseases
- Reduce premature mortality from non-communicable diseases
- Strengthen the prevention and treatment of substance abuse

---

50. United Nations General Assembly Resolution, "Transforming Our World," 12.
51. Presbyterian Ministry at the United Nations, "Study & Devotional Guide."
52. Presbyterian Ministry at the United Nations, "Study & Devotional Guide."

- Ensure universal access to sexual and reproductive health-care services
- Reduce hazardous chemical contamination and air, water, and soil pollution
- Provide access to affordable essential medicines and vaccines
- Strengthen early warning and management of national and global health risks[53]

Finally, the first global monitoring report commemorating the 10th year anniversary of the launch of the closing the gap initiative was published in 2018.[54] The report concluded that:

> Because of the pervasive and growing inequalities worldwide, there is an emerging trend towards promoting and monitoring government actions on the social determinants of health. Yet few existing indicators adequately capture a government's intent to and implementation of policies and programs to address social determinants of health. Many challenges exist to developing such indicators, some of which have been described here (e.g., those related to data availability). While the methods presented in this paper extend the state of the art in measuring government action on social determinants of health, future efforts should attend to the existing gaps to create a strong set of indicators for monitoring social determinants of health in high- and low-income countries alike.[55]

The authors of this report ultimately expect that this new set of indicators will enable policy-makers to track progress in addressing the social determinants of health and to build the evidence base of effective actions for reducing health inequities. Future global monitoring reports will be produced every three years.

Summary and Conclusion

Most of us have a highly developed sensitivity for what is right and fair. And we usually let other people know when they violate our shared obligation to behave justly. Social justice broadens our obligations as citizens who are

---

53. Presbyterian Ministry at the United Nations, "Study & Devotional Guide," 16–17.
54. Working Group for Monitoring Action, "Towards a Global Monitoring System."
55. Working Group for Monitoring Action, "Towards a Global Monitoring System," 11.

jointly responsible for the common good. Doing justice, though, is more than following social norms and obligations. It is about how we treat one another. Our interests center on distributive and procedural justice.

There are paradoxes in how we understand and practice justice. Whereas legal justice is egalitarian, partiality is necessary in the administration of procedural justice. The Universal Declaration on Human Rights is a comprehensive and global commitment to a socially just world. Doing justice means sorting out what belongs to whom and returning it to them. When making things right calls for reallocating social goods and power, those who have more than their fair share often seek to defend and protect their privileged position and resources. Only a shared sense of responsibility for each other's welfare will overcome this inequality of privilege.

Economic inequality and poverty distort and undermine our sense and practice of justice. They compromise our commitment to fairness and justice and present serious social justice challenges. Fortunately, great progress has been made and we've learned how to end economic inequality and poverty. We just need to finish the journey.

Achieving environmental justice is proving to be elusive. Research reveals significantly disproportionate environmental risks for poor and marginalize individuals and societies. The unjust distribution of environmental threats, costs, and benefits even impacts our quality of life. Fortunately, we have strong environmental laws; unfortunately, they are enforced all too seldom. Renewed resolve, commitment, and action are needed by everyone, including ourselves and our congregations, to correct our huge array of persistent and elusive distributional and procedural environmental injustices. It will help to link our environmental problem-solving efforts to the fight against other social injustices such as climate change, global health, energy shortages, and women's empowerment.

Fortunately, one of these other social justice challenges, global health equity, appears achievable in our generation. Health inequities are unfair, avoidable, and remediable differences in health status between countries and between different groups of people within the same country. Significant progress in overall world health has been made in recent decades even as significant health inequities still exist. Risks for disease, ill-health, and death remain significantly higher in poor nations and among people in lower socioeconomic classes. The World Health Organization believes that social justice is a matter of life and death and calls for urgent action. And it summons all the people of the world to live into its bold aspiration of achieving global health equity within a generation.

The five guidelines presented in this chapter identify ways that doing justice leads to better relationships. And we've discovered ways that practicing social justice has the power to transform our relationships for the better in our congregations and everyday lives.

Practical Applications

1. Think of an individual or social injustice that you find particularly perplexing and challenging. Examine what has gone wrong and consider what would make things right. What elements of distributive and procedural injustice are apparent, if any?

2. Identify evidence that economic inequality and poverty distort or undermine our sense and practice of justice. On which challenges has there been significant progress?

3. What do you think needs to happen to end poverty and economic inequality? What might you and your congregation do?

4. In what ways do you think such arts as literature, music, digital video, and cinema can promote social justice? Identify ways they have done so in your life and in that of your congregation. How about ways they can do so in the future?

5. Why do you think environmental injustice is so persistent and environmental justice is so elusive? What can you and your congregation do to help overcome environmental injustice, both in term of distributional and procedural justice?

6. Do you and your congregation share the World Health Organization's aspiration that global health equity is achievable in a generation? Look over their recommendations and action areas, and then decide which are most important, realistic, and feasible for you and for your congregation to pursue.

7. Review the United Nations sustainable development agenda goals for 2030 relating to global health equity, and the specific actions to ensure healthy lives and promote well-being for all at all ages. Then select one or two steps you and your congregation can take to help achieve global health equity in your lifetime.

For Further Study

Brueggemann, Walter, Sharon Parks, and Thomas H. Groome. *To Act Justly, Love Tenderly, Walk Humbly: An Agenda for Ministers* (Eugene, OR: Wipf & Stock, 1997).

DiAngelo, Robin. *White Fragility: Why It's So Hard for White People to Talk About Racism* (Boston: Beacon, 2018).

Goza, Joel Edward. *America's Unholy Ghosts: The Racist Roots of Our Faith and Politics* (Eugene, OR: Cascade, 2019).

Harvey, Jennifer. *Dear White Christians: For Those Still Longing for Racial Reconciliation*, 2nd ed. (Grand Rapids, MI: Eerdmans, 2020).

Kendi, Ibram X. *How to Be an Antiracist* (New York: One World, 2019).

Marshall, Chris. *The Little Book of Biblical Justice: A Fresh Approach to the Bible's Teachings on Justice* (New York: Good Books, 2005).

Presbyterian Ministry at the United Nations, "Study & Devotional Guide: Sustainable Development Goals," 2nd ed., September 23, 2019, at: https://www.presbyterianmission.org/resource/study-devotional-guide-for-the-sustainable-development-goals/

Reisch, Michael, ed. *The Routledge International Handbook of Social Justice* (New York: Routledge, 2016).

Rosling, Hans, Ola Rosling, and Anna Rosling Ronnlund. *Factfulness: Ten Reasons We're Wrong About the World—and Why Things Are Better Than You Think* (New York: Flatiron, 2018).

United Nations General Assembly. Transforming Our World: the 2030 Agenda for Sustainable Development, Resolution 70/1 (New York: United Nations, 2015).

Wilkerson, Isabel. *Caste: The Origins of Our Discontents* (New York: Random House, 2020).

World Health Organization. Closing the Gap in a Generation: Health Equity Through Action on the Social Determinants of Health. Final report of the Commission on Social Determinants of Health (Geneva, Switzerland: World Health Organization, 2008).

World Health Organization. Rio Political Declaration on Social Determinants of Health (Geneva, Switzerland: World Health Organization, 2011).

Bibliography

Anderson, Bernhard W. *Understanding the Old Testament*. 3rd ed. New Jersey: Prentice-Hall, 1975.

Bass, Diana Butler. *Grateful: The Transformative Power of Giving Thanks*. New York: HarperOne, 2018.

Batson, C. Daniel, et al. "Empathy and Altruism." In *The Oxford Handbook of Positive Psychology*, edited by Shane J. Lopez and C. R. Snyder, 417–26. 2nd ed. New York: Oxford, 2009.

Bluhm, Robyn. "Gender and Empathy." In *The Routledge Handbook of Philosophy of Empathy*, edited by Heidi L. Maibom, 377–87. New York: Routledge, 2017.

Boehm, Julia K., and Sonja Lyubomirsky. "The Promise of Sustainable Happiness." In *The Oxford Handbook of Positive Psychology*, edited by Shane J. Lopez and C. R. Snyder, 667–77. 2nd ed. New York: Oxford, 2009.

Brueggemann, Walter. "Voices of the Night—Against Injustice." In *To Act Justly, Love Tenderly, Walk Humbly*, by Walter Brueggemann et al., 5–28. Eugene, OR: Wipf & Stock, 1997.

Cameron, C. Daryl. "Compassion Collapse: Why We Are Numb to Numbers." In *The Oxford Handbook of Compassion Science*, edited by Emma M. Seppala et al., 261–71. New York: Oxford University Press, 2017.

Cameron, Kim. "Organizational Compassion: Manifestations Through Organizations." In *The Oxford Handbook of Compassion Science*, edited by Emma M. Seppala et al., 421–34. New York: Oxford University Press, 2017.

Carroll, Noel. "Empathy and Painting." In *The Routledge Handbook of Philosophy of Empathy*, edited by Heidi L. Maibom, 285–94. New York: Routledge, 2017.

Carter, C. Sue, et al. "The Roots of Compassion: An Evolutionary and Neurobiological Perspective." In *The Oxford Handbook of Compassion Science*, edited by Emma M. Seppala et al., 173–87. New York: Oxford University Press, 2017.

Cassell, Eric J. "Compassion." In *The Oxford Handbook of Positive Psychology*, edited by Shane J. Lopez and C. R. Snyder, 393–404. 2nd ed. New York: Oxford University Press, 2009.

CBS News. "'Unbelievable' Act of Sportsmanship," May 1, 2008. https://www.cbsnews.com/news/unbelievable-act-of-sportsmanship/.

BIBLIOGRAPHY

Chapman, Gary D., and Paul E. White. *The 5 Languages of Appreciation in the Workplace: Empowering Organizations by Encouraging People*, rev. and updated. Chicago: Northfield, 2012.

Clarke, Cheryl. "By Its Absence: Literature and the Attainment of Social Justice Consciousness." In *The Routledge International Handbook of Social Justice*, edited by Michael Reisch, 480–91. New York: Routledge, 2016.

Cohn, Michael F., and Barbara L. Fredrickson. "Positive Emotions." In *The Oxford Handbook of Positive Psychology*, edited by Shane J. Lopez and C. R. Snyder, 13–24. 2nd ed. New York: Oxford University Press, 2009.

Condon, Paul, and David DeSteno. "Enhancing Compassion: Social Psychological Perspectives." In *The Oxford Handbook of Compassion Science*, edited by Emma M. Seppala et al., 287–98. New York: Oxford University Press, 2017.

Cooperrider, David L., et al. *Appreciative Inquiry Handbook: For Leaders of Change*. 2nd ed. Brunswick, OH: Crown Custom, 2008.

Coplan, Amy. "Introduction." In *Empathy: Philosophical and Psychological Perspectives*, edited by Amy Coplan and Peter Goldie, ix–xlvii. New York: Oxford University Press, 2014.

Cousineau, Tara. *The Kindness Cure: How the Science of Compassion Can Heal Your Heart & Your World*. Oakland, CA: New Harbinger, 2018.

Cozolino, Louis. *The Neuroscience of Human Relationships: Attachment and the Developing Social Brain*. 3rd ed. New York: Norton, 2017.

———. *The Neuroscience of Psychotherapy: Healing the Social Brain*. 3rd ed. New York: Norton, 2017.

The Dalai Lama. *An Open Heart: Practicing Compassion in Everyday Life*. Edited by Nicholas Vreeland. New York: Back Bay, 2001.

———. *How to Be Compassionate: A Handbook for Creating Inner Peace and a Happier World*. Edited and translated by Jeffrey Hopkins. New York: Atria, 2011.

Davidson, Richard J. "The Four Keys to Well-Being." *Greater Good Magazine*, March 21, 2016. https://greatergood.berkeley.edu/article/item/the_four_keys_to_well_being

Davis, Donald E., et al. "Relational Humility." In *Handbook of Humility: Theory, Research, and Applications*, edited by Everett L. Washington Jr. et al., 105–18. New York: Routledge, 2017.

Davis, Mark H. "Empathy, Compassion, and Social Relationships." In *The Oxford Handbook of Compassion Science*, edited by Emma M. Seppala et al., 299–316. New York: Oxford University Press, 2017.

Decety, Jean, and Andrew N. Meltzoff. "Empathy, Imitation, and the Social Brain." In *Empathy: Philosophical and Psychological Perspectives*, edited by Amy Coplan and Peter Goldie, 58–81. New York: Oxford University Press, 2014.

Denham, Alison E. "Empathy and Moral Motivation." In *The Routledge Handbook of Philosophy of Empathy*, edited by Heidi L. Maibom, 227–41. New York: Routledge, 2017.

Dworkin, Ronald. *Taking Rights Seriously*. Cambridge, MA: Harvard University Press, 1978.

Ekman, Paul. "Global Compassion: A Conversation Between the Dalai Lama and Paul Ekman." In *The Compassionate Instinct: The Science of Human Goodness*, edited by Dacher Keltner et al., 274–82. New York: Norton, 2010.

Emmons, Robert A., and Michael E. McCullough, eds. *The Psychology of Gratitude*. New York: Oxford University Press, 2004.

Ekman, Paul, and Eve Ekman. "Is Global Compassion Achievable?." In *The Oxford Handbook of Compassion Science*, edited by Emma M. Seppala et al., 41–49. New York: Oxford University Press, 2017.

Fadiman, Clifton, ed. *The Little, Brown Book of Anecdotes*. Boston: Little, Brown and Co., 1985.

Feldman, Christina. *Boundless Heart: The Buddha's Path of Kindness, Compassion, Joy, and Equanimity*. Boulder, CO: Shambhala, 2017.

Figley, Charles R., and Kathleen Regan Figley. "Compassion Fatigue Resilience." In *The Oxford Handbook of Compassion Science*, edited by Emma M. Seppala et al., 387–97. New York: Oxford University Press, 2017.

Fook, Jan. "Social Justice and Critical Theory." In *The Routledge International Handbook of Social Justice*, edited by Michael Reisch, 160–72. New York: Routledge, 2016.

Fritzell, Johan. "Health Inequality and Social Justice." In *The Routledge International Handbook of Social Justice*, edited by Michael Reisch, 339–52. New York: Routledge, 2016.

Gilbert, Paul. *The Compassionate Mind: A New Approach to Life's Challenges*. London: Robinson, 2013.

Gilbert, Paul, and Jennifer Mascaro. "Compassion Fears, Blocks and Resistances: An Evolutionary Investigation." In *The Oxford Handbook of Compassion Science*, edited by Emma M. Seppala et al., 399–418. New York: Oxford University Press, 2017.

Goetz, Jennifer L., and Emiliana Simon-Thomas. "The Landscape of Compassion: Definitions and Scientific Approaches." In *The Oxford Handbook of Compassion Science*, edited by Emma M. Seppala et al., 3–15. New York: Oxford University Press, 2017.

Goldin, Philippe R., and Hooria Jazaieri. "The Compassion Cultivation Training (CCT) Program." In *The Oxford Handbook of Compassion Science*, edited by Emma M. Seppala et al., 237–45. New York: Oxford University Press, 2017.

Gordon, Kristina Coop et al. "Forgiveness in Couples: Divorce, Infidelity, and Couples Therapy." In *Handbook of Forgiveness*, edited by Everett L. Worthington Jr., 407–22. New York: Routledge, 2005.

Gray, Mel et al. "Social Justice Feminism." In *The Routledge International Handbook of Social Justice*, edited by Michael Reisch, 173–87. New York: Routledge, 2016.

Groome, Thomas H. "Walking Humbly With Our God." In *To Act Justly, Love Tenderly, Walk Humbly: An Agenda for Ministers*, Walter Brueggemann et al., 44–65. Eugene, OR: Wipf & Stock, 1997.

Haidt, Johnathan. "Wired to Be Inspired." In *The Compassionate Instinct: The Science of Human Goodness*, edited by Dacher Keltner et al., 86–93. New York: Norton, 2010.

Hamington, Maurice. "Empathy and Care Ethics." In *The Routledge Handbook of Philosophy of Empathy*, edited by Heidi L. Maibom, 262–72. New York: Routledge, 2017.

Harvey, Jennifer. *Dear White Christians: For Those Still Longing for Racial Reconciliation*. 2nd ed. Grand Rapids, MI: Eerdmans, 2020.

Haugh, Sheila, and Tony Merry, eds. *Rogers' Therapeutic Conditions: Evolution, Theory and Practice*. Vol. 2, *Empathy*. Monmouth, UK: 2001.

Hoffman, Martin L. *Empathy and Moral Development: Implications for Caring and Justice*. New York: Cambridge University Press, 2001.

Hollan, Douglas. "Empathy Across Cultures." In *The Routledge Handbook of Philosophy of Empathy*, edited by Heidi L. Maibom, 341–52. New York: Routledge, 2017.

Howell, James C. *What Does the Lord Require? Doing Justice, Loving Kindness, Walking Humbly*. Louisville: Westminster John Knox, 2012.

John, Eileen. "Empathy in Literature." In *The Routledge Handbook of Philosophy of Empathy*, edited by Heidi L. Maibom, 306–16. New York: Routledge, 2017.

Johnson, Jeri-Lynn. *The Kindness Handbook: When You Want to Help But Don't Know What to Do*. Salt Lake City: Shadow Mountain, 2001.

Johnstone, Gerry, ed. *A Restorative Justice Reader*. 2nd ed. New York: Routledge, 2013.

Johnstone, Gerry, and Daniel W. Van Ness, eds. *Handbook of Restorative Justice*. New York: Routledge, 2011.

Kauppinen, Antti. "Empathy and Moral Judgment." In *The Routledge Handbook of Philosophy of Empathy*, edited by Heidi L. Maibom, 215–26. New York: Routledge, 2017.

Keltner, Dacher. "The Compassionate Instinct." In *The Compassionate Instinct: The Science of Human Goodness*, edited by Dacher Keltner et al., 8–15. New York: Norton, 2010.

Kennett, Jeanette. "Empathy and Psychopathology." In *The Routledge Handbook of Philosophy of Empathy*, edited by Heidi L. Maibom, 364–76. New York: Routledge, 2017.

Kim, Seon-Mi, and Margaret Sherrard Sherraden. "The Capability Approach and Social Justice." In *The Routledge International Handbook of Social Justice*, edited by Michael Reisch, 202–15. New York: Routledge, 2016.

King, Philip J. "Micah." In *The Jerome Biblical Commentary*. Vol. 1. Edited by Raymond Edward Brown et al., 283–89. New Jersey: Prentice-Hall, 1968.

Kirby, James N. "Compassion-Focused Parenting." In *The Oxford Handbook of Compassion Science*, edited by Emma M. Seppala et al., 91–105. New York: Oxford University Press, 2017.

Kirkpatrick, Thomas G. *Communication in the Church: A Handbook for Healthier Relationships*. Lanham, MD: Rowman & Littlefield, 2016.

Kleinbeck, Alaina. "Practicing Kindness in the Midst of Rage." *Faith and Leadership*, October 30, 2018. https://www.faithandleadership.com/alaina-kleinbeck-practicing-kindness-midst-rage

Klimecki, Olga M., and Tania Singer. "The Compassionate Brain." In *The Oxford Handbook of Compassion Science*, edited by Emma M. Seppala et al., 109–20. New York: Oxford University Press, 2017.

Kobut, Heinz. *How Does Analysis Cure?* Edited by Arnold Goldberg. Chicago: University of Chicago Press, 1984.

Koopmann-Holm, Birgit, and Jeanne L. Tsai. "The Cultural Shaping of Compassion." In *The Oxford Handbook of Compassion Science*, edited by Emma M. Seppala et al., 273–85. New York: Oxford University Press, 2017.

Kuehn, Robert R. "Environmental Justice." In *The Routledge International Handbook of Social Justice*, edited by Michael Reisch, 319–38. New York: Routledge, 2016.

Large, Jerry. "Laws Pile Up Against Homelessness." In *The Seattle Times* newspaper, May 11, 2015, B7.

Lavelle, Brooke D. "Compassion in Context: Tracing the Buddhist Roots of Secular, Compassion-Based Contemplative Programs." In *The Oxford Handbook of Compassion Science*, edited by Emma M. Seppala et al., 17–25. New York: Oxford University Press, 2017.

Lavelle, Brooke D., et al. "A Call for Compassion and Care in Education: Toward a More Comprehensive Prosocial Framework for the Field." In *The Oxford Handbook of*

Compassion Science, edited by Emma M. Seppala et al., 475–85. New York: Oxford University Press, 2017.

Leach, Mark M., and Adebayo Ajibade. "Spiritual and Religious Predictors, Correlates, and Sequelae of Humility." In *Handbook of Humility: Theory, Research, and Applications*, edited by Everett L. Washington Jr. et al., 192–204. New York: Routledge, 2017.

Lipman, Victor. "66% Of Employees Would Quit If They Feel Unappreciated," April 15, 2017. https://www.forbes.com/sites/victorlipman/2017/04/15/66-of-employees-would-quit-if-they-feel-unappreciated.

Lustbader, Wendy. *Counting on Kindness: The Dilemmas of Dependency*. New York: Free Press, 1991.

Maguire, Daniel C. "Religious Influences on Justice Theory." In *The Routledge International Handbook of Social Justice*, edited by Michael Reisch, 27–38. New York: Routledge, 2016.

Maibom, Heidi L. "Affective Empathy." In *The Routledge Handbook of Philosophy of Empathy*, edited by Heidi L. Maibom, 22–32. New York: Routledge, 2017.

———. "Introduction: (Almost) Everything You Ever Wanted to Know about Empathy." In *Empathy and Morality*, edited by Heidi L. Maibom, 1–40. New York: Oxford University Press, 2014.

———. "Introduction to Philosophy of Empathy." In *The Routledge Handbook of Philosophy of Empathy*, edited by Heidi L. Maibom, 1–9. New York: Routledge, 2017.

Marshall, Chris. *The Little Book of Biblical Justice: A Fresh Approach to the Bible's Teachings on Justice*. New York: Good Books, 2005.

Marshall, Christopher D. *Beyond Retribution: A New Testament Vision for Justice, Crime, and Punishment*. Grand Rapids, MI: Eerdmans, 2001.

Martin, Daniel, and Yotam Heineberg. "Social Dominance and Leadership: The Mediational Effect of Compassion." In *The Oxford Handbook of Compassion Science*, edited by Emma M. Seppala, et al., 495–506. New York: Oxford University Press, 2017.

Mascaro, Jennifer, et al. "Cognitively Based Compassion Training: Gleaning Generalities from Specific Biological Effects." In *The Oxford Handbook of Compassion Science*, edited by Emma M. Seppala et al., 247–57. New York: Oxford University Press, 2017.

McCraty, Rollin, and Doc Childre. "The Grateful Heart: The Psychophysiology of Appreciation." In *The Psychology of Gratitude*, edited by Robert A. Emmons and Michael E. McCullough, 23–55. New York: Oxford University Press, 2004.

McLaughlin, Eugene et al., eds. *Restorative Justice: Critical Issues*. Thousand Oaks, CA: Sage, 2003.

Mikulincer, Mario, and Phillip R. Shaver. "Adult Attachment and Compassion: Normative and Individual Difference Components." In *The Oxford Handbook of Compassion Science*, edited by Emma M. Seppala et al., 79–89. New York: Oxford University Press, 2017.

Morton, Adam. "Empathy and Imagination." In *The Routledge Handbook of Philosophy of Empathy*, edited by Heidi L. Maibom, 180–89. New York: Routledge, 2017.

Neafsey, John. *Act Justly, Love Tenderly: Lifelong Lessons in Conscience and Calling*. Maryknoll, NY: Orbis, 2016.

Neff, Kristin, and Christopher Germer. "Self-Compassion and Psychological Well-being." In *The Oxford Handbook of Compassion Science*, edited by Emma M. Seppala et al., 371–85. New York: Oxford University Press, 2017.

BIBLIOGRAPHY

Nelson, Noelle C., and Jeannine Lemare Calaba. *The Power of Appreciation: The Key to a Vibrant Life*. Hillsboro, OR: Beyond Books, 2003.

Nordstrom, Todd. "79% of Employees Quit Because They're Not Appreciated," September 19, 2017. https://www.inc.com/todd-nordstrom/79-percent-of-employees-quit-because-theyre-not-app.html.

O'Connell, Maureen H. *Compassion: Loving Our Neighbor in an Age of Globalization*. New York: Orbis, 2009.

Parks, Sharon. "Love Tenderly." In *To Act Justly, Love Tenderly, Walk Humbly: An Agenda for Ministers*, Walter Brueggemann et al., 29–43. Eugene, OR: Wipf & Stock, 1997.

Pavlovitz, John. "The Death of Empathy in America," December 20, 2017. https://johnpavlovitz.com/2017/12/20/empathy-america-obituary/

Peterson, Christopher, and Nansook Park. "Classifying and Measuring Strengths of Character." In *The Oxford Handbook of Positive Psychology*, edited by Shane J. Lopez and C. R. Snyder, 25–34. 2nd ed. New York: Oxford University Press, 2009.

Piff, Paul K., and Jake P. Moskowitz. "The Class-Compassion Gap: How Socioeconomic Factors Influence Compassion." In *The Oxford Handbook of Compassion Science*, edited by Emma M. Seppala et al., 317–30. New York: Oxford University Press, 2017.

Porter, Steven L., et al. "Religious Perspectives on Humility." In *Handbook of Humility: Theory, Research, and Applications*, edited by Everett L. Washington Jr. et al., 47–61. New York: Routledge, 2017.

Presbyterian Ministry at the United Nations, "Study & Devotional Guide: Sustainable Development Goals." 2nd ed. September 23, 2019. https://www.presbyterianmission.org/resource/study-devotional-guide-for-the-sustainable-development-goals/

Rank, Mark R. "Why Poverty and Inequality Undermine Justice in America." In *The Routledge International Handbook of Social Justice*, edited by Michael Reisch, 436–47. New York: Routledge, 2016.

Reamer, Frederic G. "Social Justice and Criminal Justice." In *The Routledge International Handbook of Social Justice*, edited by Michael Reisch, 269–85. New York: Routledge, 2016.

Reisch, Michael, ed. *The Routledge International Handbook of Social Justice*. New York: Routledge, 2016.

Robinson, Jenefer. "Empathy in Music." In *The Routledge Handbook of Philosophy of Empathy*, edited by Heidi L. Maibom, 293–305. New York: Routledge, 2017.

Rohr, Richard. "The Source of Action," December 16, 2018. https://cac.org/the-source-of-action-2018-12-16

Rosa, William, et al., eds. *A Handbook for Caring Science: Expanding the Paradigm*. New York: Springer, 2019.

Rosling, Hans, et al. *Factfulness: Ten Reasons We're Wrong About the World—and Why Things Are Better Than You Think*. New York: Flatiron, 2018.

Rost, Stacy. "Doug Baldwin: New Anthem Policy Highlights 'Tone-Deafness' Between NFL and Players," May 25, 2018. http://sports.mynorthwest.com/457599/doug-baldwin-new-anthem-policy-highlights-tone-deafness-between-nfl-and-players/?

Ruberton, Peter M., et al. "Boosting State Humility via Gratitude, Self-Affirmation, and Awe: Theoretical and Empirical Perspectives." In *Handbook of Humility: Theory, Research, and Applications*, edited by Everett L. Worthington Jr. et al., 260–72. New York: Routledge, 2017.

Sakamoto, Izumi. "The Use of the Arts in Promoting Social Justice." In *The Routledge International Handbook of Social Justice*, edited by Michael Reisch, 463–79. New York: Routledge, 2016.

BIBLIOGRAPHY

Shoemaker, David. "Empathy and Moral Responsibility." In *The Routledge Handbook of Philosophy of Empathy*, edited by Heidi L. Maibom, 242–52. New York: Routledge, 2017.
Sim, Gerald. "Social Justice and Cinema." In *The Routledge International Handbook of Social Justice*, edited by Michael Reisch, 502–12. New York: Routledge, 2016.
Skwara, Alea C., et al. "Studies of Training Compassion: What Have We Learned; What Remains Unknown?." In *The Oxford Handbook of Compassion Science*, edited by Emma M. Seppala et al., 219–36. New York: Oxford University Press, 2017.
Spaulding, Shannon. "Cognitive Empathy." In *The Routledge Handbook of Philosophy of Empathy*, edited by Heidi L. Maibom, 13–21. New York: Routledge, 2017.
Stadler, Jane. "Empathy in Film." In *The Routledge Handbook of Philosophy of Empathy*, edited by Heidi L. Maibom, 317–26. New York: Routledge, 2017.
Steindl-Rast, David. "Gratitude as Thankfulness and as Gratefulness." In *The Psychology of Gratitude*, edited by Robert A. Emmons and Michael E. McCullough, 282–89. New York: Oxford University Press, 2004.
Stewart, John. *Personal Communicating and Racial Equity*. Dubuque, IA: Kendall Hunt, 2016.
Sturt, David, et al. *Appreciate: Celebrating People, Inspiring Greatness*. Salt Lake City: O.C. Tanner Institute, 2017.
Sullivan, Dennis, and Larry Tifft, eds. *Handbook of Restorative Justice: A Global Perspective*. New York: Routledge, 2015.
Suttie, Jill. "Compassion Across Cubicles." In *The Compassionate Instinct: The Science of Human Goodness*, edited by Dacher Keltner et al., 133–39. New York: Norton, 2010.
Swaink, James E., and S. Shaun Ho. "Parental Brain: The Crucible of Compassion." In *The Oxford Handbook of Compassion Science*, edited by Emma M. Seppala et al., 65–77. New York: Oxford University Press, 2017.
Ta, Vivian P., and William Ickes. "Empathic Accuracy." In *The Routledge Handbook of Philosophy of Empathy*, edited by Heidi L. Maibom, 353–63. New York: Routledge, 2017.
Tangney, June Price. "Humility." In *The Oxford Handbook of Positive Psychology*, edited by Shane J. Lopez and C. R. Snyder, 483–90. 2nd ed. New York: Oxford University Press, 2009.
Taylor, Jowi. "Music and Social Justice." In *The Routledge International Handbook of Social Justice*, edited by Michael Reisch, 492–501. New York: Routledge, 2016.
Toussaint, June Price, and Jon R. Webb. "The Humble Mind and Body: A Theoretical Model and Review of Evidence Linking Humility to Health and Well-Being." In *Handbook of Humility: Theory, Research, and Applications*, edited by Everett L. Washington Jr. et al., 178–91. New York: Routledge, 2017.
Tracy, Jessica L., et al. "Pride: The Fundamental Emotion of Success, Power, and Status." In *Handbook of Positive Emotions*, edited by Michele M. Tugade, et al., 294–310. 2nd ed. New York: Guilford, 2014.
Umbreit, Mark, and Marilyn Peterson Armour. *Restorative Justice Dialogue: An Essential Guide for Research and Practice*. New York: Springer, 2011.
United Nations General Assembly Resolution adopted on September 25, 2015, "Transforming Our World: the 2030 Agenda for Sustainable Development." https://www.un.org/en/development/desa/population/migration/generalassembly/docs/globalcompact/A_RES_70_1_E.pdf

BIBLIOGRAPHY

Universal Declaration of Human Rights. https://www.un.org/en/universal-declaration-human-rights/

Van Tongeren, Daryl R., and David G. Myers. "A Social Psychological Perspective." In *Handbook of Humility: Theory, Research, and Applications*, edited by Everett L. Worthington Jr. et al., 150–64. New York: Routledge, 2017.

van Wormer, Katherine S., and Lorenn Walker, eds. *Restorative Justice Today: Practical Applications*. Thousand Oaks, CA: Sage, 2013.

Wade, Nathaniel G., et al. "But Do They Work? A Meta-Analysis of Group Interventions to Promote Forgiveness." In *Handbook of Forgiveness*, edited by Everett L. Worthington Jr., 423–39. New York: Routledge, 2005.

Weng, Helen Y., et al. "The Impact of Compassion Meditation Training on the Brain and Prosocial Behavior." In *The Oxford Handbook of Compassion Science*, edited by Emma M. Seppala et al., 133–46. New York: Oxford University Press, 2017.

Wilkerson, Isabel. *Caste: The Origins of Our Discontents*. New York: Random House, 2020.

Wolff, Florence I., and Nadine C. Marsnik, *Perceptive Listening*. 2nd ed. New York: Harcourt Brace Jovanovich, 1993.

Working Group for Monitoring Action on the Social Determinants of Health, "Towards a Global Monitoring System for Implementing the Rio Political Declaration on Social Determinants of Health: Developing a Core Set of Indicators for Government Action on the Social Determinants of Health to Improve Health Equity," September 5, 2018. https://equityhealthj.biomedcentral.com/articles/10.1186/s12939-018-0836-7

World Conference on Social Determinants of Health, Rio De Janeiro, Brazil, October 19–21, 2011, "Rio Political Declaration on Social Determinants of Health." https://www.who.int/sdhconference/declaration/Rio_political_declaration.pdf?ua=1

World Health Organization, "Closing the Gap in a Generation: Health Equity Through Action on the Social Determinants of Health." In the Commission on Social Determinants of Health Final Report. Geneva, Switzerland: World Health Organization, 2008.

World Health Organization, "Global Monitoring of Action on the Social Determinants of Health: A Proposed Framework and Basket of Core Indicators," 2016. https://www.who.int/social_determinants/consultation-paper-SDH-Action-Monitoring.pdf?ua=1

World Health Organization press release, "Inequities Are Killing People on Grand Scale." https://www.who.int/mediacentre/news/releases/2008/pr29/en/

Worline, Monica C., and Jane E. Dutton, "How Leaders Shape Compassion Processes in Organizations." In *The Oxford Handbook of Compassion Science*, edited by Emma M. Seppala et al., 435–56. New York: Oxford University Press, 2017.

Worthington Jr., Everett L. "Political Humility: A Post-Modern Reconceptualization." In *Handbook of Humility: Theory, Research, and Applications*, edited by Everett L. Washington Jr. et al., 76–90. New York: Routledge, 2017.

Worthington, Everett L., Jr., et al. "Epilogue: What We Have Learned, Where We Are Likely To Go." In *Handbook of Humility: Theory, Research, and Applications*, edited by Everett L. Worthington Jr. et al., 343–55. New York: Routledge, 2017.

Worthington, Everett L., Jr., et al. "Introduction: Context, Overview, and Guiding Questions." In *Handbook of Humility: Theory, Research, and Applications*, edited by Everett L. Washington Jr. et al., 1–15. New York: Routledge, 2017.

BIBLIOGRAPHY

Wronka, Joseph. "Human Rights As Pillars of Social Justice." In *The Routledge International Handbook of Social Justice*, edited by Michael Reisch, 216–26. New York: Routledge, 2016.

Zehr, Howard. *The Little Book of Restorative Justice*. New York: Good Books, 2015.

Zehr, Howard, and Barb Toews, eds. *Critical Issues in Restorative Justice*. Boulder, CO: Lynne Rienner, 2010.

Zimbardo, Philip G., et al. "Heroism: Social Transformation Through Compassion in Action." In *The Oxford Handbook of Compassion Science*, edited by Emma M. Seppala et al., 487–93. New York: Oxford University Press, 2017.

About the Author

Thomas G. Kirkpatrick is an educator, pastor, trainer, writer, and consultant with specialties in relational communication, small group ministries, and conflict management. He is the author of the Roman & Littlefield Alban publications *Communication in the Church: A Handbook for Healthier Relationships* and *Small Groups in the Church: A Handbook for Creating Community*. He has been an adjunct professor at the University of Dubuque Theological Seminary, pastor of Westminster United Presbyterian Church, Galena, Illinois, and associate pastor of Little Church on the Prairie Presbyterian Church, Lakewood, Washington. Previously, he was associate professor of speech communication at Whitworth University in Spokane, Washington. He has also served as a campus minister and a program director of camps and conferences. He received his MA and PhD from the University of Washington, DMin from San Francisco Theological Seminary, MDiv from Fuller Theological Seminary, and BMusEd from the University of Oregon. He lives with his wife, also a PCUSA minister, in Maple Valley, Washington, and his four children live in Portland, Oregon; Albany, Oregon; La Crosse, Wisconsin; and Snohomish, Washington.

You can reach him at his website at www.tomkirkpatrick.org.

Index

acceptance, 7, 14, 17, 20, 40, 55, 65, 85, 108
Ames, Kevin, 97
Amos, 15
Anderson, Bernhard W., 15
appreciate, 5, 11, 30–33, 62, 81, 87–94, 96–97, 99–101
    art, 30, 44
    compassionate acts, 62
    humility, 9
    kind words, 79
appreciation, ix–xii, 3, 12, 53, 66, 75–76, 79
    affirmation and, 5
    as obligation, 88, 101
    as valuing, 88, 101
    benefits of, 93, 101
    culture of, 97, 102
    define, 88, 99
    energy of, 89–90, 94–96
    expressing, xi–xii, 79, 87–88, 91, 93, 97–99, 101–2
    feeling, 89, 97–98
    genuine, 87
    lack of, 93, 96–97, 102
    language of, 98, 101–2
    of one another, 91
    power of, 90, 93, 96, 98, 101
    practice, 94, 102
    research, 88, 93, 96, 98
    show, 92, 94
Appreciative Inquiry, 99–100, 102

Baldwin, Doug, 34
Baez, Joan, 112
Bass, Diana Butler, 90n5, 102
Beckstrand, Gary, 97
best practices, 2, 17, 20, 40, 47, 71, 74, 85, 88, 96, 101, 104
biblical references
    1 Corinthians 13:4, 73
    Deuteronomy 6:4–5, 3
    Isaiah 1:17, 103
    Matthew 9:36, 46
    Matthew 22:37–40, 3
    Micah 6:8, 1, 14
    Romans 12:15, 19
    1 Thessalonians 5:11, 87
Black Lives Matter, x
Bloomberg, Michael, 36
Bluhm, Robyn, 32
brain
    activate, 23
    chemistry, 54, 83
    circuits, 82
    development, 54, 65
    incentive and resource-seeking system, 53, 53n13
    left and right, 21
    networks, 75
    patterns, 54
    plasticity, 65, 78
    sequencing, 3
    shape, 52–54, 70
    signal, 53

INDEX

brain *(continued)*
    soothing and contentment system, 53, 53n13, 57, 65
    threat and self-protection system, 53, 53n13, 66n41
    trigger, 53, 85
    wired, 52–53, 70, 76
Brueggemann, Walter, 15, 108
Buddha, 85
Buddhism, 9, 48, 48n1
Buddhist, 23, 52n10, 64, 66, 68, 74, 84
Buddhist tradition, 66, 84

Calaba, Jeannine Lemare, 89
Cameron, C. Daryl, 63, 92n7
caring, 36, 41, 52–53, 57, 59–60, 70–71, 80, 103, 107
    community, 40, 78, 103
    genuine, 17, 75
    instinct, 77
    lifestyle, 26
    process, 25–26, 26n12, 44
    role, 59
    science, 26n11
    sense, 28
Cassell, Eric J., 48
Cert, Bennett, 104
Chapman, Gary, 96, 98
Childre, Doc, 88, 92
Christian community, 21
Christianity, 9
Chung, Leeva C., 41
church, x, 25, 34, 37, 39, 41–42, 121
Cleaver, Eldridge, 112
climate change, xiii, 36, 63, 114, 123
color
    communities of, 116
    people of, 112, 114–15
communication
    behaviors, 38
    breakdowns, xi, 39, 90, 96
    careful, 38, 41
    classes, 88
    climate, 38, 44–45
    ethics, 38, 40
    healthier, 90
    monopolizing, 82

    signals, 53
    skills, 31, 40
compassion
    benefits of, 63, 71
    blocks to, 60
    capacity for, 65, 67n43, 77
    climate of, 58
    defining, 48, 49n6
    enhance, 64
    experience of, 51, 58, 71
    fatigue, 58–63, 61n30, 67, 71–72, 76
    feelings of, xi–xii, 27, 46–52, 55, 57, 60, 62–63, 66–67, 66n41, 70–71
    inhibitors, 59–60, 71–72
    justice and, 70–72, 111
    manage, 58, 61, 71–72
    numbness, 63, 71–2
    practice of, 66n41
    research, 47, 49n6, 50n8, 51n9, 52n10, 56, 57n20, 58, 61n30, 64, 64n32, 66–68, 67n43
    risk and protection factors, 59, 61–62, 71–72
    showing, ix, 47, 50–51, 53, 60, 62–64, 70–71
    skills, 65, 67n41, 72
    stress, 58–62, 61n30, 71–72
    thrive on, 52, 70, 76
    training, 54, 61–62, 64–67, 66n41, 67n43, 68, 71
compassionate
    actions, 47, 51–52, 57–58
    concern, 83
    environment, 60
    feelings, 35, 47, 63, 66
    heart, 84
    instincts, 66, 76
    mind, 68
    mind training, 54, 67n41
    organizations, 57
    outcomes, 66
    responses, 49, 57, 66, 69
    thoughts, 66
congregations, ix, 1–2, 11–12, 17–20, 25, 31, 35, 37, 39–41, 45–47, 66, 71–73, 77, 85–88, 100–4, 109, 117, 123–24

INDEX

Cousineau, Tara, 74, 76, 78
Cozolino, Louis, 48n1, 53–54, 65–66, 77
cross-cultural, 10, 52n10
cultivate
    compassion, 66–68, 72, 78
    empathy, 41
    humility, 2, 7, 13
    kindness, 14, 17, 77–78, 85–86
cultural
    boundaries, 69
    contexts, 17
    differences, 7, 41, 44
    empathy, 32, 41
    humility, 10
    interactions, 6
    relationship, 12
    research, 52n10
    rights, 107, 113
    self-determination, 113
    sensitivity, 10, 12, 16–17, 32
    worldview, 10
curiosity, 16, 26, 40–41, 56, 77–79, 83, 85

Dahlsgaard, Katherine, xi
The Dalai Lama, 46, 48, 48n2, 52, 66n41, 68n45, 74
Davidson, Richard, 82, 82n16
defensive, 11, 13, 39, 42, 56, 82, 85, 90
democracy, xiii, 36, 107, 110
Denham, Alison E., 29
DiAngelo, Robin, 113
discrimination, 25, 65, 105, 107, 116
diversity, 8, 13, 37, 40, 112
Dworkin, Ronald, 115

empathic
    ability, 61
    action, 24
    concern, 19, 23, 26–27, 30–31, 36, 40, 47, 58, 61, 64
    fatigue, 51
    listening, 31, 36, 83, 99
    processes, 32
    resonance, 47
    response, 23–24
    sensitivity, 52
    stress, 61
    style, 23
    suffering, 23
    understanding, 26, 28, 44–45
empathy
    caused by, 20
    components of, 25
    demonstrated, xi
    experiencing, xi-xii, 20, 22, 25, 31, 33, 38, 44–45, 109
    facet of, 22, 27
    feel, 23, 39
    impairment of, 31, 33, 44
    increase, 43
    lacking, 23, 33, 37
    limit or regulate, 24
    manage, 62
    moved by, 36, 104
    research, 21n3, 23, 26–27, 31–32, 33n27, 34, 43
    role of, 21n3, 26n12, 28–29, 30n22, 34, 36, 45
    show, x, 34
    training in, 24
    value of, 34, 36
environmental
    activists, 116, 120
    benefits, 114, 123
    challenges, 113, 117
    costs, 114, 123
    justice, 112–13, 116–17, 123–24
    laws, 113, 116, 123
    policies, 115–16
    risks, 115, 123
equality, 68, 107, 109–12, 120, 123–24
equanimity, 84–86
equity, 106, 111, 114, 116–19, 123–24
ethics, 20, 38, 40, 40n37, 44, 47, 51, 69, 105

faith communities, x, xii, 1, 4, 18, 103
Feldman, Christina, 84–85
Figley, Charles R., 61
flourish, xi, xiii, 5, 20, 26, 44, 47, 69–71, 74, 77–78, 81, 83, 85, 96, 101, 108
forgiveness, 6–7, 16, 27, 38, 41–44, 61, 77n10, 109

INDEX

Gates, Bill and Melinda, 36
gender, 7, 31–32, 44, 51n9, 75, 105, 118, 120
generosity, 6, 17, 58, 75, 77, 80–83, 82n16, 85, 89–90, 93
Germer, Christopher, 55, 57
Gilbert, Paul, 52–54, 53n13, 57, 60–61, 67n41, 68
global
    community, 96
    compassion, 50n8, 63, 66n41, 68, 69n53, 70
    confrontations, 91
    connected-world, 10
    health, 110–12, 116–24
    needs, 36
    statement, 107
God, 1, 3–5, 7, 14–15, 79, 108
Goetz, Jennifer L., 49, 50n6
Goza, Joel Edward, 112
gratitude, xi, 6, 13, 17, 89–90, 90n5, 94, 101
Griffin, John Howard, 112
Groome, Thomas H., 15
growth, 17, 40, 62, 65, 67, 116, 120
guidelines, xiii, 2, 17, 20, 40, 45, 47, 71, 74, 80, 85–86, 88, 101, 104, 123

Harvey, Jennifer, 109
health equity, 117–19, 123
healthy relationships, 2, 3–6, 16, 40, 81, 91, 108–9
Heineberg, Yotam, 68
Hinduism, 9
Holtman, Mallory, 34
Hosea, 15
Howell, James C., 74
humble
    attitude and behavior, 12
    be, 12, 13–14, 18
    citizens, 13
    people, 7, 12
    reaction, 9
    recognition, 10
    team member, ix
    walk, 1, 14–15, 18, 74, 108

humility
    benefits of, 12, 13n14, 18
    creates respect, 16
    definition of, 7
    makes us real, 1, 12
    practicing, xi–xii, 1–2, 4, 7, 18
    research, 5–7, 10n11, 11, 13–14, 17–18
    sense of, 8, 10n11

Ickes, William, 24n10
injustice, 103–4, 108–9
    distributive, 114–16, 124
    environmental, 113, 115, 117, 123–24
    perceived, 111
    procedural, 124
    racial, 34
    social, 117, 123–24
intercultural, 31–32, 41, 44
interpersonal
    communication, 88
    conflict, 41, 91
    environment, 65
    functioning, 10n11
    inferiority, 12
    qualities, 17
    relationships, 6, 32, 35
    self-presentation, 9
    situation, 5, 8
    well-being, 56, 68
intrapersonal, 9, 56
Irving, Debbie, 12
Isaiah, 15, 103–4
Islam, 9

Jesus, xi, 3, 46, 66n41, 82, 112
Job, 19
Judaism, 9
Judeo-Christian, xi, 3, 14, 74, 108
justice, 33, 35, 45–45, 108–11, 106
    criminal, 36, 105
    distributive, 36, 105, 114–15, 122, 124
    doing, xi–xii, 1, 14–15, 17, 74, 103–5, 107–9, 122–23
    for all, x, 110, 115, 122
    human, 96, 112

INDEX

humility related to, 17
is elusive, 112, 114–15, 117, 123–24
is relational, 105–6
legal, 104–6, 122
practice of, 123–24
principles, 107, 110
procedural, 105–6, 115–16, 122, 124
racial, 34, 109
research, 104, 113–15, 119, 123
restorative, 36, 69, 105, 105n5
retributive, 36, 69, 105, 105n5
seek, 104–5
sense of, ix, 28, 70, 105, 111
social, 13, 34, 68, 71–72, 104–7, 107n11, 109–10, 116, 118, 122–24
system, 26, 35–36, 69
threat to, 103, 109
true, 108
undermine, 109

Kauppinen, Antti, 28
Kendall, Frances E., 112
Kendi, Ibram X., 113
kindness
    acts of, 4, 52n10, 66, 73–75, 77–78, 80, 83, 109
    compassion and, 109
    define, 74
    inner, 57, 70
    instinct, 76
    justice and, 57
    lifestyle of, 81
    loving, 1, 14–15, 70, 74–75, 77, 82, 84–85, 108
    power of, 76
    practicing, 82
    showing, ix, xi–xii, 15, 73–75, 77–78, 85–86
    research, 74–75, 78
King, Philip J., 14–15
Kirkpatrick, Thomas G., 14n17, 17n25, 37, 38n36, 40n37, 41n38, 61n29, 77n10, 88n1
Kleinbeck, Alaina, 82
Kohut, Heinz, 27, 27n16
Kuehn, Robert, 114

La Guardia, Fiorello, 104–6
LGBTQ+, 37
liberation theology, 112
listening, 8, 17, 31, 36–38, 40, 43, 70, 77, 80, 83, 85, 99, 111
Lustbader, Wendy, 81

Maguire, Daniel, 105
Marshall, Chris, 106, 108
Martin, Daniel, 68
Mascaro, Jennifer, 60–61
McCraty, Rollin, 88, 92
meditation, 64, 66n41, 67, 78
Micah, xi, 1, 14
mindfulness, 56, 66, 71, 77
morality, 12, 20, 21n3, 27–29, 32, 37, 44
Morton, Adam, 24
multicultural church, 25
multiracial, 109
Muslim, 10, 112
Myers, David G., 5n4, 14

Neafsey, John, 3
Neff, Kristin, 55, 57
Nelson, Noelle, C., 89
neuroscience, 20, 23, 32, 65, 82
Nordstrom, Todd, 97

O'Brien, Keith, 69
O'Connell, Maureen, 69
openness, 3, 6, 8, 12–13, 17, 25, 38, 40, 85
oppression, 105, 108, 111
organizational, 58, 68, 97–99

pandemic, xiii, 37, 63, 75, 81, 121
Parks, Sharon, 74
Patel, Eboo, 112
patience, 4, 24, 52–53, 55, 67n41, 82–85, 109
Paul, 21, 74, 87
Pavlovitz, John, 37
peace, 11, 13, 13n14, 37, 41, 55, 64, 70, 91, 93, 110, 120
Peter, Paul, and Mary, 112
planet, 33, 73, 75, 112, 116, 120
platinum empathy, 40
Poitier, Sydney, 112

INDEX

political, 8–9, 17, 32, 36–37, 68, 76, 105, 107–9, 111, 113, 115, 119
poverty, 36–37, 109–112, 116–17, 119, 121, 123–24
practical wisdom, xiii, 47, 71, 74, 85, 88, 101, 104
privilege, 36, 60, 68, 106, 108, 112, 123

Qur'an, 10, 112

racism, xi, 112
Rank, Mark, 109–10
Rankin, Sarah, 35
Reamer, Frederic G., 105
reconciliation, 16, 43, 109
Regan, Kathleen, 61
relational, 6, 8, 11, 73
    breakdowns, xii
    contexts, 17
    ethics, 38–40, 40n37, 44
    health, 16, 17n25, 40, 43, 86
    humility, 11
    love affair, 4
    qualities, 31, 84–85
    repair, 17, 43
    researchers, 11
    satisfaction, 16–17, 26
    sensitivity, 12
    skills, 98
relationality, 69–70
religion, 7, 9–10, 15, 36, 50n8, 74–75, 112
religious, 8–9, 17
    authorities, 9
    awakening, 64
    bodies, 37
    boundaries, 69
    communities, 5, 9
    contexts, 11, 17, 32
    educator, 15
    institutions, 37
    leaders, 103, 106
    people, 7
    platitudes, 19
    respect, 9
    structure, 37
    teachings, 7

views, 10, 22
wisdom, 9
reparations, 109
Rogers, Carl, 27, 65
Rosling, Hans, 110, 118n39

self-compassion, 54–57, 57n20, 71
self-esteem, 2–4, 10n11, 22, 77, 83, 87–88, 93
self-kindness, 55
sensitivity, 6, 10–12, 16–17, 32, 52, 64, 74, 78, 83, 105, 122
Shapiro, Rami, 75
Shoemaker, David, 29–30
Simon-Thomas, Emiliana, 49, 50n6
social science, xi, 5–7, 32, 41, 49, 61n30, 66, 68, 75, 88
spiritual
    benefits, 12
    leader, 5
    people, 7
    religious and, 7
    roots, 14
    stress, 12
    support, 7
    teachers, 67n41
spirituality, 7, 64
supportive, 4, 6–7, 11–13, 17, 20, 24–28, 35, 38, 40, 44, 46, 53, 55–59, 62, 77, 80, 83–85, 89, 98, 109
Steindl-Rast, David, 89
Steyer, Tom, 36, 117
Sturt, David, 97
sustainable, 20, 68, 75, 77, 81, 83, 92, 100, 106, 119–21, 124
systemic racism, x, xiii, 111–12

Ta, Vivian P., 24n10
Tangney, June Price, 2
Theoharis, Liz, 112
thoughtfulness, 79–81, 85
thrive, 11, 52, 70, 76
Ting-Toomey, Stella, 41
transform
    attitude, 66n41
    dysfunction, 83, 86

INDEX

experience, 12, 90
feelings, 90–91, 94, 98
hurt, 71
injustice, 117
kindness, 76
lives, 44, 89, 101
motivations, 12
people, 99
planet, 73, 75
power to, xi, 4, 17, 20, 45, 47, 71, 74, 86, 88, 104, 123
practice of forgiveness, 42
relationships, ix-xiii, 2, 4, 17–20, 34–36, 44–45, 47, 64, 73–78, 83, 85, 88, 101, 104, 109, 123
resentment, 92
suffering, 69, 71
understanding, 24, 26
Tucholsky, Sara, 34

Universal Declaration of Human Rights, 107, 122
universal health care, 110, 118–19, 121

Van Tongeren, Daryl R., 14

Wallace, Liz, 34
warmth, 17, 23, 40, 52–53, 55–56, 65, 75, 85, 95
well-being, xi, 4, 6–7, 10n11, 16, 21, 23–24, 26, 39, 44, 47–48, 50–52, 54, 56, 57n20, 61, 68–71, 74, 76–77, 82, 82n16, 85–86, 96–97, 99, 101, 107n10, 119, 121, 124
White, Paul, 96, 98
Wilkerson, Isabel, 112
Wink, Walter, 112
World Health Organization, 117–18, 123–24
world religions, 9
Worthington Jr., Everett, 9, 41